# Unlocking

## *Mi*

Michael Bright is a biologist and senior producer with the BBC's world-acclaimed Natural History Unit in Bristol. He is a graduate of the University of London, a member of the Institute of Biology, and a Fellow of the Royal Entomological Society of London.

# Unlocking Nature's Secrets

*Michael Bright*

ARIEL BOOKS

BRITISH BROADCASTING CORPORATION

By the same author:
*Animal Language*

Drawings by Illustrated Arts

First published 1984 by the British Broadcasting Corporation
35 Marylebone High Street London WIM 4AA

Typeset by Phoenix Photosetting, Chatham
Printed in England by Mackays of Chatham Ltd

This book is set in 10/11 Ehrhardt Linotron

ISBN 0 563 20322 6

# Contents

# Introduction

Often in science a key discovery, a new theory, a fresh concept, an advance in technology, or a chance encounter, provides a launching-pad for an understanding of nature's mysteries. Just as a row of dominoes falls after the first one is pushed, so too in science, a particularly timely and apposite development may trigger a series of remarkable revelations.

In 1953, for instance, a race ended. It was the race to unravel the structure of a complex organic molecule with the tongue-twisting name of deoxyribonucleic acid (DNA), a chemical substance that was thought to carry the information of heredity in the genes, a blueprint containing all the information necessary to make living things – 'the stuff of life'. A paper appeared in the scientific journal *Nature* with the title 'Molecular Structure of Nucleic Acids'. It was by Francis Crick and James Watson, both then of the University of Cambridge. Using the technique of X-ray crystallography they were able to build a model of DNA. They proposed the now famous double helix and it was accepted by the scientific community. They had won the race and went on to reap the benefits of victory. More importantly, their accomplishment was a key discovery that allowed other researchers to unlock many more molecular secrets that one day may lead to a fuller understanding of the mechanisms, for instance, of cancer and other major diseases.

Crick and Watson could not have achieved their goal without the fund of knowledge that had been accumulating before them. Fritz Meischer and Emil Fischer, at the end of the nineteenth century, had proposed that the information about species' characteristics is encoded in a molecule consisting of many sub-units. This was made popular in *What is life?* by Erwin Schrödinger in 1944, and become known as the 'codescript'. In the 1930s the chain structure of polypeptides was accepted, and it was proposed that the gene is a protein. During the same period the analysis techniques were being developed. Max von Laue, a

German physicist, and his colleagues in 1912 found that an X-ray beam, passing through a crystal, would show up its structure by the patterns of interference. In Britain, W. L. Bragg and his son W. H. Bragg refined the technique, and X-ray crystallography subsequently helped research teams in molecular biology to analyse the structure of complex organic molecules. On several different fronts advances were being made. What Crick and Watson had done was to bring this all together and make a quantum leap in the understanding of the molecules of life.

In this book I explore how a handful of these kinds of advances in the natural sciences, made in the past few decades, have influenced our understanding of nature. The theory of continental drift, and plate tectonics, for example, when it was eventually accepted by the establishment, was instrumental in explaining the distribution of curiously isolated populations of plants and animals across the globe. In 'Continents on the Move' I explore the way animals as diverse as green turtles and fruit-flies have adapted their lifestyles to cope with the movement of the land masses.

The realisation that animals might possess senses beyond the perception of man, and the development of the technology with which to appreciate them, showed that almost every channel of communication open to animals and plants is actually being used. The invention of the sound spectrograph literally opened up the study of sound in nature so that we, as predominantly visual animals, can appreciate the subtleties of the way that animals use sound, in particular, to communicate with others (see *Animal Language*, BBC Publications). The arrival of the ultrasonic microphone, together with the sound spectrograph for analysis, for example, has allowed researchers to listen in to the high-frequency sound world of bats, dolphins, tree crickets and a host of small mammals. In 'Beyond Human Perception' I have chosen the dolphin's amazing ability to see and perhaps kill with sound as an example of an ultrasound user having taken its ability to an extreme.

The development of apparatus that can detect wavelengths of light outside the visual spectrum of man has revealed an entirely new world, say, in the ultraviolet range. Many insects, some nectar-feeding birds, and just recently a fish have been found to see a picture of the world that is different from our own. Flowers reflecting ultraviolet light turn out to have patterns on the petals which guide visiting insects to the nectar stores and thus ensure help in pollination. At the other end of the visual spectrum, infra-red is found to be important to some animals, for instance, to the rattlesnake for detecting prey. Even as I write, an expedition of cave scientists are exploring the Mulu Caves in Sarawak where 'squeaking' snakes, coiled around stalactites, have been seen to pluck bats and cave swiftlets from out of the air during the diurnal movement of animals in and out of the caves. How do they find the bats and birds in the dark? Could they be detecting infra-red radiations from the bodies of their prey? That is a mystery that must remain so for the time being, but another one is just beginning to be solved.

Fireflies, in reality beetles that produce their own light, have a highly complex Morse code system of communication. In 'Living Lights' I describe the kinds of messages being flashed between individuals, and go on to show how bioluminescence, as it is known, has been found to be more common than we first thought, particularly with the creatures of the deep sea.

The revelation that many animals are probably able to detect the earth's magnetic field, and use that information for orientation and navigation during migration or foraging, has opened up an enormous area of research. This may well affect the alignment of bacteria in a magnetic field, sharks' ability to navigate by the lines of magnetic field across the world, and the recent theory that whale strandings are due to whales being magnetically confused. The observations have led scientists to look for structures in the body that could facilitate such a 'Sixth Sense', and lo and behold, there they are – small particles of magnetic material found in the heads or nerve-control centres of bees, pigeons, whales, sharks, butterflies, and even man.

Our own vision of the world has also been enhanced. The development of new deep-sea submersibles has allowed marine biologists a glimpse of one of the least-explored regions on earth. In 'At the Bottom of the Sea' I report on the remarkable finds in the Pacific, where the discovery of deep-sea hydrothermal vents has revealed a whole new, and hitherto unknown, community of creatures that does not depend on the sun as a source of energy but instead harnesses the incredible heat escaping from the centre of the earth.

In 'A Change in the Weather' we find how climatological and meteorological studies have shown that short and long-term changes in atmospheric conditions can have considerable implications for the survival of life on earth. The technique of tagging animals, described in 'Individual Labels', has given us new insights that allow us to fill in some of the most extra-ordinary details of animal movements around the planet. Bird-ringing showed, for instance, that the arctic tern, the 'blue-riband' of migrants, travels from the Arctic to the Antarctic and back each year in order to take advantage of the optimum conditions for feeding and breeding. Radio collars, similarly, have enabled field biologists to follow creatures like wolves in order to fathom out their lifestyles in the remote and inaccessible areas in which they live. Even satellites in space are being used to track creatures such as polar bears and basking sharks.

Sometimes luck plays a part in scientific advancement. In 'Chance Encounters of an Earthly Kind' I reveal how un-expected discoveries often show us how much we still need to find out about our own planet. It has often been said that we know more about the moon than we do about the depths of the sea. And there are still places on land that have escaped the inquisitive gaze and destructive intervention of man.

There is one other criterion that I have adopted in the selec-tion of scientific tales to be told and that is the importance of the personalities of the researchers themselves. Millions of scientists from all over the world sit in their laboratories experimenting, analysing, checking, re-checking and publishing. Much of their work is routine and without it science would not be able to progress. Occasionally, however, scientists appear who take those quantum leaps. They are often recognised by their peers and contemporaries and receive the accolade of the international scientific community – the Nobel prize, the Royal Society medals, and other glittering prizes. There are others, who have given birth to new and exciting branches of their sciences or have pushed out significantly the bounds of understanding, but have not as yet been recognised for the 'big one'. I have chosen one scientist for whom I have a particular regard, for the simple reason that, for me, he put back the 'awe' in biology. I recall my first chance encounter. It was at the annual meeting of the American Association for the Advancement of Science in Washington. Tom Eisner was lecturing. I sat with mouth agape as discovery after discovery was presented for me to enjoy. There was a water-beetle that was in an evolutionary race with a predatory fish. The beetle exuded a spot of a nasty-tasting sub-stance that caused the fish to spit it out. The fish cottoned on to this and began to wash the beetle, by passing water to and fro in its mouth and gills, before it swallowed it. Not to be outdone, the beetle found that if it exuded its repellent slowly the fish couldn't wash it off. And so the story continued. I was fascinated, but more importantly I was hooked and ready to take on board the real message of Eisner's work. Could it be, asked Eisner, that we are interfering with nature at some subtle chemical level, thereby upsetting the natural course of events and perhaps changing our environment for the worse?

It was my first introduction to the concept of chemical ecology and it forms the first chapter in this book.

# Chemical Warfare in Nature

At the National Bureau of Standards in Gaithersburg, USA, biochemists have set up the world's first environmental-specimen bank. It contains choice morsels of human liver, marine bivalves, food grains and lichens, all to be kept as a deep-frozen historical record of environmental pollution. Unlike, say, oil pollution, many pollutants are invisible and insidious, but accumulate in appreciable amounts in certain tissues. There are the heavy metals, like lead and mercury, organochlorine pesticides like DDT, nuclear wastes, acid rain, smog, cadmium, polychlorinated biphenyls (PCBs) and so on. Millions of tonnes of pollutants are discharged into the environment every day of the year. Limits are set, controls effected and monitored in the hope that nature can cope. The catastrophic effects are too often obvious – birth defects in people and animals that have been exposed to 2–4–5T pesticides or PCB wastes; horrifying malformations in children exposed to mercury; entire lake populations disappearing and forests dying as a consequence of acid rain; and the list goes on. But what of the more hidden dangers? What do we know about the way even minute amounts of our waste materials interfere with plant and animal communities? How are we upsetting the natural world at a chemical level? Although we are vaguely aware of the importance of chemical interactions in an ecosystem, we have very little idea about their chemical vulnerability. There are, however, researchers in a scientific discipline who are attempting to gather the information. The study is called chemical ecology, and it records the way that plants and animals interact at a chemical level. As a new science, bringing together biochemists, ecologists and behavioural researchers, it is still at the fascinating stage of exploration and discovery, and one person who has been making some of those discoveries is Tom Eisner, Jacob Gould Schurman Professor of Biology, at Cornell University, in the State of New York. 'Discovery in nature is not purely a matter of chance. An *urge* to discover can increase the frequency of discovery, and the urge', suggests Tom Eisner, 'can be developed. The single prerequisite is a genuine interest in nature, which is certainly in all of us unless it has been drummed out through our early *education*.' Eisner's early education was fortunate. He was brought up by understanding parents who tolerated a bedroom so filled with pet insects 'it became a hazard to the rest of the family'. They lived in Uruguay in self-imposed exile from Hitler's Germany. Country walks took on a new dimension surrounded, as they were, by the rich flora and fauna of South America. But in those early days Eisner was nearly lost from biology. His father, a chemist, had designs on his son following the family tradition. Eisner junior compromised and settled for chemical ecology. In particular, he became fascinated by the chemical defence strategies of different types of arthropods. His inordinate fondness for high-tech beetles developed on a field trip with a close friend, E. O. Wilson. Wilson was working on ants (and already talking sociobiology), while Eisner collected beetles. 'I would pick one up and smell a discharge, but could find no references in the textbooks.' He went on to make some remarkable discoveries.

Even during a recent filming expedition in Arizona, Eisner succeeded in uncovering a mystery on the last day. With the equipment packed away, Eisner and wildlife cameraman Roger Jackman went for an evening stroll and came across a pond from which hundreds of miniature spade-foot toadlets were emerging. The tiny creatures, about 2 centimetres long, had completed their metamorphoses and were leaving the pond in synchrony. Eisner and Jackman watched as they scurried across the soft mud to the safety of the surrounding scrub. On looking more closely, Jackman noticed that some of the toads were dead or dying, and partly buried in the mud. Scattered around were gaunt or rotting carcasses bleached in the hot sun. Gingerly Eisner and Jackman pulled at the corpses with tweezers and, to their amazement, felt something, under the mud, pulling at the other end.

Careful digging failed to reveal the predator as it quickly burrowed down into the safety of the soft mud. By scooping handfuls of mud from around an unfortunate trapped toadlet they uncovered a grub-like insect larva, about the same size as the toad itself.

Back in the laboratory the predator was identified as a horsefly larva, *Tabanus punctifer* and, as luck would have it, the little creature took kindly to a terrarium. It quickly burrowed into the mud, rear end first, and would lie in wait for a suitable-sized meal to hesitate for one vital moment. Immediately the hinged mandibles, hidden just below the surface, would pinch on the leg or belly of the toadlet like grappling hooks. The skin pierced, the larva injected a slow-acting venom to suppress the toadlet's struggles, and, as the corpse was dragged into the mud, the larva would extract blood and other body fluids.

The paradox of the fly-eats-toad story is that when the spade-foot toads grow up and the horse-fly adults emerge, it is more than likely that the toad will eat the fly.

## Bombardier beetles

The star performer in Tom Eisner's entomological theatre of war is the bombardier beetle, *Brachinus*, which, perhaps, possesses the ultimate in carabid weaponry. The beetle is normally found under stones and logs near the water's edge, but when caught in the open, the bombardier is able to strike predators approaching from any angle with a boiling blast of noxious chemicals – benzoquinones – and escape to fight another day.

If an ant, for example, grabs a leg, the beetle will swivel its abdomen around in a split second and direct the jet of scalding liquid square on to the attacker, inflicting instant irritation and causing it to let go. If under constant attack, the beetle can fire twenty or thirty times to repel inquisitive predators. Eisner tried to 'prey' on the bombardier beetle himself by putting it to his mouth. The bombardier understandably took exception: 'The moment I took the beetle between the lips it discharged, and the sensation of heat was immediate and disagreeable. There was an acrid taste and a peppery burning feeling.' The discharge is accompanied by an audible report, hence the name bombardier, and appears as a little cloud of vapour from a pair of openings at the tip of the beetle's abdomen.

Research in Germany by Professor Hermann Schildkrecht revealed that the chemical spray is boiling hot, the result of an explosive oxidation process, effected by the mixing of the chemical precursors of benzoquinones, known as hydroquinones, with separately stored hydrogen peroxide, and a cocktail of enzymes in a chamber behind the tip of the abdomen. The hydrogen peroxide rapidly decomposes, releasing oxygen, which acts as the propellant, while oxidation of the hydroquinones provides the irritant.

Together with Daniel Aneshansley, a long-time friend and

colleague at Cornell, Eisner was able to place a small thermo-couple behind a firing beetle and confirm that the mixture reached 100°C, the temperature of boiling water. This work, in itself, was fascinating stuff. For one thing, there is no other example in nature of an animal generating an explosion and shooting out a poison at a high temperature. Imagine, then, the researchers' surprise when they discovered, by means of ultra-high speed filming at an incredible 4000 frames per second, that the discharge is pulsed. Instead of coming out in an even stream, the spray squirts like a machine-gun at a rate of about 500 to 1000 pulses per second. Eisner reasoned that the beetle is achieving a greater spray impact by pulsing the jet, but more importantly, it does not blow off its own behind. The pulsed nature of the reaction stops any overheating in the explosion chamber.

After the initial discovery with bombardier *Brachinus*, Eisner came across other bombardier species with interesting defence systems. 'I was in Panama, and picked up some beetles there, which the moment I touched gave off a sound, and I felt heat in the tips of my fingers from the spray they were ejecting.' Return-ing to the laboratory with live specimens, Eisner found that they have the same hot and explosive discharge as *Brachinus* in response to attack but deliver it in a different way. The spray gland openings are spaced out on each side, near the tip of the abdomen and, instead of applying the spray in the right direction by waggling the abdomen, this beetle, a paussine bombardier *Goniotropis*, employs a unique principle of physics, hitherto only known to have been used by man. The principle is the Coanda effect. When milk is poured it sometimes has the annoying propensity to curl around the lip of the milk jug and on to the table-cloth – this is the Coanda effect, named after a Rumanian engineer Henri Coanda, and is the tendency for gases or liquids to follow the curvature of a solid. In the case of the paussine beetle there is a flange on either side of the abdomen, next to the propulsive gland openings. If the insect is under assault at the front end, the jet of fluid can bend a full 50°C, following the curve of the body, and thereby be deflected into an accurate forward direction. The flange acts as the deflector. The abdo-men can be twisted slightly to deal with attackers from the side or rear, but is not flexible enough to fire forwards. 'We believe that this is the first example of a biological mechanism that operates on the Coanda principle,' says Eisner.

There is yet another bombardier with a more primitive system than the previous two and its discovery suggests to Eisner that he may be looking here at an evolutionary sequence. This more primitive insect, a metriine beetle, does not squirt out a poisonous fluid but simply lets it boil out from under the flanges of the wings that cover the gland openings on each side. During an attack the beetle froths in a bubbling mass of boiling secretion, the bursting bubbles sending tiny droplets of chemicals in all directions so that the animal is surrounded by vapour. This not only repels the attackers, but allows the animal to walk nonchalantly through a whole swarm of would-be predators.

The bombardier family, though, is not infallible. Bombardiers may find themselves sometimes in the webs of orb-weaving spiders. The golden silk spider, *Nephila clavipes*, for instance, will race up to its prey and try to take a bite, to be repelled immediately by the beetle's defensive spray. Orb-weavers of the genus *Argiope*, on the other hand, gingerly approach the prey, gently wrap it in a silken envelope and then let it discharge away inside until quinone supplies are exhausted, and the *coup de grâce* can be administered. Exit one bombardier.

## Cold sprays

In the Arizona desert, which Eisner describes as 'one of the most stunning areas to work in', another beetle, a tenebrionid by the name of *Eleodes*, deploys its artillery by assuming a headstand position. If disturbed, it comes to a halt, elevates its rear end and squirts a noxious mixture of cold quinones at the aggressor. It is particularly effective against spiders, ants and most small rodents. Its defence system appeared to work quite well, but as Eisner was roaming around the desert one day he noticed, scattered about here and there, remnants of beetles that gave every appearance of having been eaten by some predator. Surviving debris tended to be wing covers that are indigestible, pieces of leg, and the tip of the abdomen where the poison glands are situated. The jagged edges to the pieces were reminiscent of an attack by a mouse, so Eisner set up rodent traps. With a small collection of the local rodent fauna, experiments were set up in the laboratory. Most of the rodents would not go near the beetles, all, that is, except one: the grasshopper mouse, *Onychomys torridus*. It would approach the beetle, grab it, force the rear end into the sand where it could be safely discharged and then bite off its head.

Ploy and counterploy are common in the chemical defence

world, but some animals learn faster than others. The devil's rider *Anisomorpha buprestoides*, an orthopteran walking-stick, can deter predators such as blue jays *Cyanocitta cristata* even before they attack. A well-aimed spray, powerful enough for Eisner and his colleagues to need gas masks when handling the insect, is released from gland openings on the thorax. One approach is sufficient to prevent the birds from coming back for more. The South American mouse oppossum *Marmosa demararae* was not put off so easily. Having learned the first time with a faceful of irritating spray, the mouse opossum returned, grabbed the insect with a front paw, and held it behind its back while it discharged the rest of the secretion. The walking-stick, its armoury spent, was decapitated and eaten.

## The clockwork beetle

The most engaging, perhaps, of Eisner's creatures, a miniature chrysomelid beetle with the gigantic name of *Hemisphaerota cyanen*, is found in Florida. For twenty-five years a small patch of pine and palmetto has drawn Eisner back each year to become one of his favourite study areas. One day he noticed the little beetle, smaller than a ladybird, moving across a palmetto. 'It looked', recalled Eisner, 'like a tiny flat-footed clockwork toy – a joy to watch as it marched up and down the palm.' But the palmetto highway is often overrun with ants which see the little fellow not as a charming little insect to be watched and admired but as an easy meal to be taken back to the nest. *Hemisphaerota*, though, knows how to deal with ants. It can fly away, which is inconvenient as it has to unwrap its wings from under the wing covers; it can drop to the ground which might mean going from the frying-pan to the fire; or it can clamp down limpet-fashion, on to the palmetto. And when *Hemisphaerota* clings to the leaf almost nothing can shift it.

Eisner was intrigued. Huge battalions of marauding ants would push and heave at the tiny shell, but all to no avail. It would not budge. Occasionally an ant was able to prise a mandible under the edge of the shell but still *Hemisphaerota*, with legs and antennae safely tucked away, kept its hold. Suction clearly was not the mechanism being used. The clue, it turned out, was in the big feet.

Meanwhile back in the laboratory ... *Hemisphaerota* was subjected to microscopic examination, which revealed that the soles of its feet are made up of thousands of bristles. Higher magnification showed that each bristle is forked with two apparent suction cups at the end; these later proved not to be used as such. Instead, the pads of bristles are moistened with an oily secretion that oozes out from glands at the base of the bristles and on to the tips. A thin layer of oil is squeezed between the pad and the leaf, thus securing the beetle by adhesion. (Two glass plates with water between them will demonstrate the principle.) By attaching a pulley and a weight to one specimen Eisner and Aneshansley were able to demonstrate that *Hemisphaerota*'s 60,000 adhesive pads could withstand the force of a 2-gram weight, the equivalent of a human holding up 200 grand pianos. When danger is past, the beetle detaches the pads at one point and then removes each foot as if peeling off sticky-tape. While it ambles along unmolested only a few bristles make contact with the leaf surface. If you get it to clamp on to glass you can see the minute droplets of oil left behind, a relatively small loss, in fact less than 0.005 per cent of body weight, for such an effective defence strategy.

So far, Eisner has found only one predator capable of outwitting *Hemisphaerota*, and that's one of the assassin bugs, *Aribus cristatus*, known locally as the wheel bug. The bug extends its proboscis, which is equipped with venom, and probes for a point of weakness under the margin of the beetle. If it is successful, the bug injects a nerve poison. The beetle's knee joint, which has been pressing the pads to the substrate, relaxes and it can be turned over and the juicy parts eaten.

The story, though, does not end there, for *Hemisphaerota* has another trick up its sleeve, or in the case of the larva, on its back. The Oscar for the 'most extraordinary defence system used by an insect' must surely go to this creature that recycles its own waste and protects itself with a faecal shield. Strings of faecal pellets are curved over the larva's back, each string guided to its precise position to form an impregnable cover. Amazingly, Eisner found that if a small piece of the shield is chipped away the larva can somehow detect the loss and adjust the curvature of the next few strings of faeces to fill in the gap.

Another beetle, *Cassida rubiginosa*, has adopted a similar system and carries a package of cast larval skins and faeces on a moveable fork-like protuberance at the tip of the abdomen. The directable shield can be deployed to parry the thrust of formicid mandibles, to act as a parasol against dessication, and to keep off the rain.

The larva of the green lacewing *Chrysopa slossonae* is partial to the woolly alder aphid *Prociphilus tesselatus*, and has adopted a similar 'defensive-parasol' strategy to fool the aphids' ant guard. The *Chrysopa* larva plucks the white waxy fluff from the aphids and places it on its own back, taking about twenty minutes to disguise itself. Thus it is protected from attack by the ants and can feed unmolested in the aphid colony.

## Borrowed poisons

Insects sometimes make poisons themselves from suitable raw materials or they acquire them from other sources. Many plants manufacture defence substances, such as alkaloids or phenols, but some herbivorous insects are not only insensitive to them but can also appropriate them for their own defence. The larvae of several species of Australian saw-flies utilise *Eucalyptus* oils. They are guarded by their mother until they have taken in enough oil from the *Eucalyptus* leaves to fend for themselves. Ingested nutrients from the leaves pass to the stomach, while the resins are somehow separated and diverted to pouches in the foregut and stored. During the day the larvae remain in a rosette-shaped group, heads facing outwards, and when threatened vomit simultaneously. If pursued, individuals will bend their heads backwards and dab regurgitated oils on to their backs. The smell is enough to put off the most ardent of attackers, even before they are close enough to bite. Any oil left on the mouthparts is reingested. When the larvae pupate, oils stored in the pouch, which in the last instar constitutes 20 per cent of the body, are incorporated into the pupal case.

In the Northern Hemisphere the pine forests are denuded by the pine saw-fly larva *Neodiprion sertifer*. The larvae eat the needles and chew holes in the twigs, but when attacked, arch their backs right over and secrete a droplet of repellent directly on to the attacker. The repellent is regurgitated pine resin. The pine saw-fly, in the same way as its Australian counterpart, has appropriated the defence substances of the host plant for its own use.

The same goes for *Apiomeris*, the camphor assassin bug, which likes camphorweed. Very few insects can tolerate camphorweed for the leaves and stalks are covered with minute droplets of sticky camphor resin. Undeterred, *Apiomeris* collects the droplets with its front legs, wipes the secretion on to the middle legs, and with the hind legs, plasters the resin all over its underside. This laborious and painstaking task is carried out by the female. When she lays her eggs, each one is liberally smothered with camphor to protect it from insect-egg predators.

In Mexico and California, millions of monarch butterflies *Danaus plexippus* overwinter in dense colonies on the trunks of trees, protected from most bird predators by bitter-tasting heart poisons, called cardenolides. These were acquired from milk-weed plants at the larval stage of development. Some butterflies mimic the monarch's bright colours and attain a certain amount of protection. There are, however, some birds that have become tolerant to the poisons. Researchers Linda Fink, now at Cornell, and Florida University's Lincoln Brower, came across flocks of black-backed orioles *Icterus abeillei* and black-headed grosbeaks *Pheucticus melanocephalus* that were picking off the butterflies without a care for the cardenolides. The researchers found that the monarchs in Mexico vary considerably in their degree of unpalatability. The orioles were seen to taste the butterflies, reject the strongly poisonous ones, and swallow the others; the grosbeaks just ate the lot.

The moth, *Utetheisa*, appropriates the poisonous resources of a legume but, as so often seems to be the case, there is an un-expected twist to the story. The seeds of the plant contain potent alkaloid poisons and are the targets for the *Utetheisa* caterpillars. What has proved interesting to Eisner is that the caterpillars actively compete for access to the seeds, chewing their way through the pod and eating the whole seed. With many cater-pillars on a plant, some are able to collect a lot of poison and others very little. The poison is retained through pupation and into the adult.

*Utetheisa* is a day-flying moth, conspicuously coloured in red, white and yellow. The colours warn predators that it is nasty to eat. Eisner checked this by offering scrub jays *Aphelocoma coeurlescens* a choice of juicy, edible insects and adult *Utetheisa* moths. The brightly coloured *Utetheisa* were totally ignored – a perfect protection. But there was more to come.

Later research revealed that the alkaloids are also an important part of courtship rituals. A male moth performs a courtship 'dance' in front of the female, fluttering close to her head. High-speed photography was used to isolate the moment of contact, and Eisner was able to see that two 'brushes' are splayed at the moment of contact and a secretion passed from the male to the female. Closer examination revealed that the substance oozes out from tiny pores, and chemical analysis showed that it is the same alkaloid eaten by the caterpillar earlier in the life cycle. *Utetheisa* uses the poison, both as predator repellent and as an aphrodisiac attractant. Eisner began to speculate: is the female evaluating the quality of her mate by the amount of poison he contains?

Males raised on an alkaloid-free diet were placed in an arena, together with poisonous males and normal females. The female initiated courtship by climbing a stem and wafting a sexual attractant down wind. The male picked up the scent, homed in on the female, and commenced his fluttering dance. Throughout the tests the females were more likely to mate with the poisonous males, which led Eisner to conclude that the poisonous alkaloid is an important ingredient in the sexual selection process of *Utetheisa*. The females appeared to be favouring the males that could best store the poisonous alkaloid, an ability likely to have been inherited, and so beneficial to any offspring. The caterpillars that were the best poison-collectors, at the competitive larval stage, became the best available mates as adults. In short, they have a better chance of survival.

## Lubber grasshopper

In the southern USA there is a grasshopper that seems not to behave as grasshoppers should. Most grasshoppers are fast-moving, but the lubber grasshopper, *Romalea microptera*, is large, flightless and slow. When under attack, as a first-strike strategy, it hisses and froths, both from the thorax and the mouth. Air from the respiratory system or trachea, mixes with the defence chemicals, causing them to foam. The thousands of tiny bubbles burst and release a fine cloud of repellent around the creature's body. If the predator is not deterred, the grasshopper's second line of defence is activated and it vomits a particularly offensive slurry from its mouth. Most predators make off rapidly.

The lubber grasshopper was interesting to Eisner in that it took him into a controversial area of study. For many years he has been concerned with chemical pollutants. Eisner is probably more aware than most that even small amounts must upset some biological system, somewhere, at some time. Just consider, for instance, the minute amounts of sex pheromone a moth needs to find its mate, or the few molecules of the smell of jam that attract a wasp to the picnic. The way that man discharges new substances, from pesticides to fertilisers, and from heavy metals to nuclear waste, into the natural world must be upsetting the ecological balance. Those animals that rely on chemicals for communication or defence, for example, are going to be silenced. *Romalea* came into the story because Eisner, and colleagues in the Chemistry Department at Cornell, isolated a chlorinated phenol in the regurgitated froth, which they thought may have been derived from a herbicide eaten by the insect. This would have been the first instance of the secondary use of a pesticide released by man, and an example of the way nature has a nasty habit of picking up discrepancies in the environment and turning them to her advantage, which need not be to the benefit of man. The story, since, has taken a slight twist for the better in that ticks have been found to produce chlorinated phenols, seemingly quite naturally. Nevertheless, the hiccup did focus attention on one possible consequence of emptying chemicals across the planet.

## Millipede mysteries

Millipedes, hard-bodied cousins of the insects, possess chemical defences and one species, *Apheloria corrugata*, is particularly well protected. For many years it was noticed that an attack on *Apheloria* was often accompanied by the smell of bitter almonds. Eisner and his co-workers noticed that when this millipede was threatened it would coil up into a tight spiral and nothing would dare go near it. They surmised that some kind of chemical is being given off, and discovered that it is none other than hydrogen cyanide. How, though, does the millipede itself survive in its own pool of poisonous gas? As is often the case in science, one solution gives rise to a million questions and, as yet, that one is still to be answered.

Eisner has noticed that when he picks up certain millipedes a brownish fluid weeps from the body of the creature. Analysis of the exudation has shown it to be composed of quinones. Interestingly, where the fluid touches Eisner's skin little tanned spots appear, and in this observation he has been able to deduce a likely evolutionary history for these kinds of chemical defence systems.

Each time an insect or a millipede moults its skin in order to grow, quinones are used for tanning, to toughen the exoskeleton. Arthropods clearly had the basic chemicals as part of a genetic heritage; all they needed to do was develop the ability to contain the active ingredients and devise a discharge mechanism to deliver the goods. Eisner takes the argument even further: 'One of the nice prerogatives we have as biologists is that we can always go back in evolution and speculate, and there is no way you can test these ideas experimentally.' He suggests that the use of quinones for the tanning process is in itself already a biochemical specialisation.

Many arthropods and plants produce the chemical precursors of quinones in their body fluids. When the organism is damaged, the precursors are oxidised into quinones at the site of the injury. There they act both as disinfectants and as tanning agents which form a protective scab. Eisner postulates that, in the course of evolution, when the ancestors of arthropods did not have a tough outer skeleton, the antiseptic quinones were already there to effect a tanning process.

Millipedes have turned out to be a surprising bunch of animals, little studied and little understood. One of the 'pill' millipedes, for instance, produces little droplets of sticky fluid much like other millipedes but from glands opening along the middle of the back. But there the similarity ends, for when these creatures are caught and bitten by, say, a wolf spider, the spider is paralysed instantly, and for some considerable time afterwards. Alkaloids that work on the nervous system of the predator were found in the fluid. This was of interest to Eisner, as an example of a chemical system in nature which could conceivably be helpful to man. 'Anything that has an effect on the nervous system', suggests Eisner, 'is, at the very least, interesting from a pharmacological point of view. It's an open frontier.'

The amounts of defence chemicals stored by millipedes can be quite formidable – up to 7 per cent of its body weight can be stored by a single individual. One mystery animal, however, is not impressed. In the State Park, near Cornell University, there is a thriving population of millipedes. Eisner would visit them often, but noticed that if he went early in the morning he would find dozens writhing on the ground. Closer inspection revealed that their heads were missing. In this particular species the head and the first few segments after the head lack the defensive glands. Some predator in the park had hit upon the idea of decapitating the millipedes and feeding on the heads only.

Eisner and his team trapped mice, shrews and a whole host of small animals in an attempt to unmask the assassin. All were repulsed by the millipedes' chemicals. 'Robespierre', as it came to be called, eluded Eisner: 'That bandit is still out there on the loose, and we consider him our friendly competitor who has a biological secret which is a mystery to this day.'

## Daddy-long-legs

The familiar long-legged arachnids, known as harvestmen or daddy-long-legs, that live on the forest floor in leaf litter, and on tree trunks and fallen logs, have been found to employ a unique chemical defence. Eisner and another long-time colleague and chemist, Jerrold Meinwald, examined one phalangid, *Vonones sayi*, and found that it had a two-level defence. In the company of ants, *Vonones* would just freeze and go unnoticed. If, however, it was detected and attacked, it would exude a fluid which clearly irritated and repelled the assailants. Closer inspection revealed the nature of the offensive material – again, a collection of quinones.

One of the problems facing animals that make use of quinones is that they are unstable in water and therefore cannot be stored for any appreciable length of time. *Vonones* solves this by storing the active ingredient and the solution in which it is delivered, separately. The quinones are produced in glands along the margins of the body, but the watery solution is regurgitated from the mouth.

When an ant attacks, two droplets of the clear regurgitate appear at the mouth and are transferred along a groove to the gland openings between the first and second legs. A brown substance, the quinone cocktail, is added to the droplets from the glands. *Vonones* then places the tips of its front legs into the mixture and, with a series of rapid strokes, paints the ant. The ant retreats. Eisner and Meinwald found that, although *Vonones* has very small glands, it nonetheless is able to produce sufficient quinones to defend itself against a prolonged engagement of over 1500 individual attacks.

## Vinegaroons

The nocturnal whip scorpions are probably the oldest group of living arachnids. Fossils, not very different in shape and structure from present-day 'vinegaroons', have been found in sediments over 300 million years old. They get their colloquial name from the vinegar-like spray they produce when disturbed. Eisner's first encounter with them was in Arizona in 1959 and, together with Ralph Ghent, he brought them back to Cornell, where they flourished in captivity and were subjected to a series of tests.

*Mastigoproctus giganteus*, as its name suggests, is big – up to 65 millimetres long – with eight legs, a pair of pincer-like claws at the front end and a whip-like protuberance on the tip of the abdomen (opisthosoma). It is similar, but not closely related, to a true scorpion, lacking the dangerous sting but still well equipped to defend itself. At the tip of the abdominal portion are two glandular openings fed by large muscular-walled glands. The slit-like openings are located at the base of the whip. It is this base that does the revolving, much like a modern gun emplacement, although, if an attack comes directly from the front, the entire abdomen must be brought around to facilitate accurate discharge. The spray can be ejected as far as 60 centimetres. In tests, ants, grasshopper mice, lizards, birds and a conveniently available armadillo were successfully repelled. The researchers went back to the wild.

During the daytime whip-scorpions hide under rocks or bury themselves in the sand, venturing forth at night to hunt in identifiable foraging territories, and returning to the same rock or crevice at dawn. Possibly their most powerful adversary is another arachnid – the solipugid or sun spider, a 70 millimetre long creature with grasping pedipalps designed to seize prey, backed up by a set of enormous crushing pincers that tear it apart. But, despite the formidable weaponry, *Mastigoproctus* dodged the energetic advances of the solipugids, repelling them with its well-aimed spray.

The spray itself is composed mostly of acetic acid – about 84 per cent, according to the analyses carried out by Jerrold Mienwald and Alastair Monro. At that concentration it is evidently very powerful as a deterrent. But, there is a problem. Acetic acid, surprise, surprise, is not the entire story, for many of the creatures being sprayed are hard-bodied invertebrates, protected by their exoskeletons. How is it that the acetic acid can penetrate their outer covering to effect the irritation?

Arthropod exoskeletons are built in two layers – the hard skeletal part which gives form and rigidity to the body, and the outer waxy layer which prevents both dessication and waterlogging. In order to break through the outer layer the whip-scorpion has incorporated a powerful solvent in its spray. It is called caprylic acid, and Meinwald and Monro found just 5 per cent in a spray sample. The same principle is used in the formulation of commercial insecticide sprays.

### Little bleeders

Blister beetles 'bleed' from joints in their legs when disturbed. Contact with the beetle causes small blisters to appear on human skin, hence the name. Analysis of beetle blood samples, many years ago, revealed the blistering agent to be cantharidin, otherwise known as 'Spanish fly', a substance brought from the Middle East at the time of the Crusades and used as a medicinal compound. It was also reputed to be an aphrodisiac on account of its mildly irritant properties at low doses and its ability to cause, as the French chemist Meynier once put it, 'erections dourloureuses et prolonguées'. At high doses it is a vertebrate nerve poison, as several ill-fated and disillusioned Don Juans found to their cost. It was popular, at both dose levels, in Italy at the time of the Borgias.

Self-imposed bleeding or auto-haemorrhaging in beetles was found by Eisner, and co-worker James Carrel, to be subject to a certain degree of self-control. An attack by an ant on one leg of a beetle results in bleeding from that leg only. Squeezing the entire body with forceps initiates a more general reaction with bleeding from all limbs, and sometimes other joints.

Tests showed cantharidin to be an effective repellent. Beetles placed in an arena close to the entrance of the laboratory's pet ant colony were first approached by the ants but left well alone when bleeding started. Voracious ground beetles enticed to have a go at the blister beetles were similarly rebuffed. Certain preying mantids, asilid flies, mirid bugs, and ant-lion larvae, however, could cope with the self-induced, sanguineous display and ate the beetles up. Why, we have no idea.

Ladybirds (Coccinellidae) 'bleed', as do the bloody-nosed beetles, *Timarcha* spp., and both groups are conspicuous in their environment – the ladybirds are spotted either red and black or yellow and black, and the bloody-nosed chrysomelid beetles exude bright-red blood from their mouth parts, against a jet-black body. Poison extracted from one chrysomelid – the larvae of the leaf beetle *Diamphidia locusta* – by the South African bushmen of the Kalahari is used for preparing poisoned arrows. The larvae of the Mexican bean beetle *Epilachna varivestris* 'bleeds' from broken spines, and the female oil beetle *Meloë proscarabaeus* of Europe 'bleeds', oozing a distasteful thick fluid from the leg joints.

## All gummed up

Entanglement with tacky threads and sticky sprays appears to have evolved many times as a means of defence in terrestrial invertebrates. The Malayan ant *Pachyconcyla tridenta*, for example, will shoot out a thread of foam at an aggressor up to a distance of 100 millimetres. The ant waves the thread from side to side, ensnares the attacker, and then runs off before it can get free. Other ants, though, are usually on the receiving end.

Earthworms, slugs and terrestrial flatworms have a slimy coat that deters ants by gumming up their mouthparts and legs.

Cockroaches, *Blatta* spp., produce a defensive slime on the upper side of the abdomen. The slime solidifies on the attacker, and it is stuck to the ground, unable to break the thread.

A very primitive creature, *Peripatus* – almost a midway stage between worms and arthropods and assigned to a phylum of its own called the Onychophora – sprays a sticky fluid from two glands on its head. Any predator, such as an ant or centipede, is totally immobilised, as the substance hardens very quickly on contact with air.

The larvae of syrphid flies like to eat aphids. The adult lays her eggs near an aphid colony and the emerging youngsters gobble up the aphids at a tremendous rate. Unfortunately, this idyllic lifestyle is likely to be upset by the arrival of a bunch of highly aggressive ants. Ants 'tend' aphids, much as we look after cows, for the honeydew they produce. The aphids are 'milked' by the ants and, in return, receive protection. Quite understandably, the ants take umbrage at syrphid larvae rustling the herd, and weigh in with their acid sprays and tough, biting mandibles. The larvae munch on unperturbed. When bitten they simply arch their backs and dab a droplet of a viscous fluid on to the ant's mandibles. The ant lets go, visibly distressed, and backs away.

Termites can also deal with ants. The Australian termite, *Nasutitermes exitiosus*, for example, has two methods of defence at its disposal. The workers have strong mandibles and can grasp invading ants and even crush them. Sometimes the workers simply grab the attacker and anchor it to the spot until a soldier termite is able to come along and deal with it.

The soldier termites of this species, known as nasute soldiers, have pointed nozzles at the front of the head. From there a sticky, entangling spray is discharged which will quickly immobilise an ant or a centipede. Irritants in the spray cause the attacker to scratch or attempt to wipe away the offending material, only to get further glued up. Also contained in the spray is a chemical message which summons help. This alarm pheromone is effective for up to 30 millimetres, and serves to recruit more nasute soldiers to gather around the attacker. If a soldier is touched, it responds by spraying. If the enemy remains lively, the soldiers stay put. As soon as it shows signs of giving up, the soldiers retire.

Termites are an interesting bunch of creatures. Sometimes referred to as 'white ants', they are really social cockroaches. Termite soldiers, as defenders of the colony, have become walking weapon systems. Several researchers, including Glenn Prestwich and David Wierner, who worked with Meinwald at Cornell, André Quennedey, of the University of Dijon, and Jean Deligne of the Free University of Brussels, have discovered that termites have evolved a variety of tactics to incapacitate or confuse an enemy.

A simple bite can be more than it seems. In some species, for example, glands on the front of the head discharge anticoagulants and toxins into the wound, and an attacker can be successfully deterred and perhaps even killed. Soldiers of *Macrotermes* species have this system. When under attack, usually from ants, the soldiers become extremely active and begin to warm up. The metabolic heat generated causes a waxy secretion from the frontal gland to flow like oil, so that each bite is accompanied by the fatal cocktail. Substances in the secretion not only stop the ant's blood from coagulating, but also soften the cuticle around the puncture, thus deactivating the ant's cuticle repair mechanism.

*Rhinotermites* soldiers have a peculiar 'paintbrush' at the front of the head with which they daub a spot of contact poison on to an aggressor. The chemical structure of the secretion is such that it works rather like a poisoned arrow. There is a chemical that penetrates the attacker's waxy cuticle, and another which, once inside, is toxic.

Perhaps the most peculiar defence system is utilised by a species of self-sacrificing termite that does not have a soldier caste. Each *Ruptitermes* worker has a constricting muscle around a reservoir of defensive secretions contained within its abdomen. When attacked, the termite contracts the muscle, ruptures at a weak joint in the abdomen wall, and blows itself apart, spraying an unpleasant sticky mixture, which also includes an alarm pheromone, all over the assailant.

## On the cushion of death

The sundew plant *Drosera* is carnivorous. It eats little flies for breakfast. Any unfortunate insect that comes into contact with the sticky, glandular hairs will be entangled and trapped, and gradually digested. That is, all except one – the moth *Trichoptilus parvulus*. It is a plume moth and its secret is on its wings. Plume moths are characterised by the feathery plumes on the edges of each wing. If a moth flies into the sticky glands of the sundew the feathery plume is discarded and left on the plant while the moth escapes. With this ability to cheat the sundew, *Trichoptilus* found a vacant ecological niche. The plant understandably has few parasites, and so the moth has adopted the sundew as the food plant for its larvae. The larvae not only get their meal but are also afforded protection.

The larvae are virtually invisible during the day but emerge at night to feed on the glandular stalks, and occasionally even eat the remains of flies that have been trapped by the plant. The longer glands at the edge of the leaf are left until last, effectively protecting the larvae against marauding ants and centipedes. A larva can move about freely on and around the glands with the help of bristles along its body. Only the tips of the bristles come into contact with the glue and they can easily be withdrawn from the fluid as the larva moves along.

## Attack and defence

To end this chapter I would like to quote two stories that have not emerged from the Cornell laboratories, but are so intriguing, I could not have left them out.

The first is another story of insect defence. Tina White and John Weaver, entomologists at Clemson University, South Carolina, discovered that the caterpillar of the moth *Cerura borealis*, which is related to the European puss moth, wriggled when presented with certain musical notes. It was almost as if it were dancing. The key frequencies were found to be between 330 and 360 Hertz, which is roughly E to F sharp above middle C. The clue to this dance came when the research duo noticed that some of their specimens had been parasitised by a wasp which had laid its eggs below the skin of the caterpillar, leaving the hatching larvae to eat their way through the living host. The wings of the minute wasps, it was found, emitted a sound with a pitch around about the note of F. The sound of this note was enough to trigger the caterpillars into their defensive postures.

One of the striking features of the *Cerura* larva is a collection of tentacles at its rear end. During the dance, filaments covered with thousands of projections produce formic acid. As the tentacles are flicked, the caterpillar protects itself by discouraging the approaching wasp with a cloud of formic acid.

The second story is unusual for it is an instance (and very few have been recognised) where an insect controls the behaviour of another by the use of an allomone.

The larvae of the berothid lacewings, *Lomamyia latipennis*, live in the nests of the termite *Reticulitermes hespurus*, and in those nests alone. In Solano County, California, where both insects are found, *Lomamyia* has a choice of the nests of two other species of termite but, as J. B. Johnson and K. S. Hagen, of the University of California at Berkeley discovered, it prefers *Reticulitermes hespurus*. Indeed, it has a special relationship with *R. hespurus* that prevents it from living anywhere else.

A cursory examination of the termite nest and its berothid interlopers often reveals a state of seemingly happy coexistence, the larvae moving freely among the termites without threats or fights. When a larva is ready to feed, however, the climate changes.

A young larva, much smaller than the termite workers, approaches a termite and wriggles its abdomen in front of the termite's head. The termite makes no effort to escape and just stands there apparently transfixed. After a couple of minutes it falls over paralysed. When all movement has ceased the berothid larva eats it. Older and larger larvae dispense with the wriggle and produce so much of the toxin that they can knock out six workers at a time.

When offered any other species of termite, or other insects, the larvae were unable to perform. The aggressive use of the chemical is specific to one type of termite. Synthesis of the substance, interestingly, may afford a new and effective method of controlling termite pests.

'Chemical ecology', Eisner once wrote, 'is a field in which exploration and discovery are still very much in order, for the very fundamentals are still vague. At the very root of the matter is a need for an expanded knowledge of how individual organisms function as chemists – what substances they employ, how they employ them, and why.'

At his Cornell laboratory a dedicated team of researchers have been trying to find out the answers, and in their quest have uncovered some of the most bizarre and fascinating stories that nature has allowed us the privilege of observing. Let us hope that these revelations in some way help to underline the need for an understanding of living sytems, at very basic levels, so that future generations may see them too.

# Beyond human perception

In his *Stroll through the World of Animals* in 1934, the Hamburg naturalist Baron Jakob Johann von Uexküll suggested that each creature on this planet lives in an *Umwelt* – its own sensory world evolved to satisfy its own particular requirements.

The eighteenth-century Italian naturalist Lazzaro Spallanzini was puzzled, for instance, by the way bats could fly about in the dark, but it was not until 1938 that Donald Griffin, the American zoologist, discovered that bats are able to find their way by using very high frequency sounds. The French naturalist, Jean-Henri Fabre, postulated in 1879 that female emperor moths attract a mate by wafting scent into the air. Eighty years later, researchers at the Max Planck Institute isolated the active ingredient from silk moths. It became known as a pheromone. Karl von Frisch, the Austrian Nobel prize-winner and eminent ethologist, found that bees not only see in colour, but also respond to ultraviolet light, a colour denied to humans. (See Chapter 3).

Since these discoveries, many mysteries have been solved when scientists have found that animals are using environmental cues quite beyond normal human perception. Frequently the pioneers had been close to their goal but were thwarted because they did not have the means to detect the signals. During the technological revolution of the past few decades we have come to realise what visionaries some of these early naturalists were.

Often as not the behaviour under examination was concerned with animal communication, and fundamental problems that any animal will have are due to the constraints of the environment in which it is living. To overcome these limitations, and to ensure that the message gets through, many animals have gone to the limits of their chosen medium.

**A most subtle perfume**
On the morning of 6 May 1879, on the laboratory table in the home of Jean-Henri Fabre, a female peacock emperor moth

emerged from its chrysalis. It is the largest of the European moths, with a wing-span of about 150 millimetres, and so, besotted with her size and beauty, Fabre kept the moth under observation in a bell-jar. Later that night, just as the household was retiring to bed, one of the children, 'little Paul', came running in great excitement. 'Come quickly, come and see the moths, big as birds. The room is full of them.'

The family rushed to the room to find it under siege. Fabre wrote: 'One of the windows in the laboratory had been left open. We enter the room, candle in hand. What we see is unforgettable. With a soft flick-flack the great moths fly around the bell-jar, alight, set off again, come back, fly up to the ceiling and down. . . . The scene suggests a wizard's cave with its whirls of bats. Little Paul holds my hand tighter than usual, to keep up his courage.'

And for several nights afterwards the same thing happened, always between eight and ten o'clock, when it was overcast and pitch black outside, and always male moths.

This aroused Fabre's curiosity. What could it be that attracted the males from afar to join the female? In the inky darkness it couldn't be a visual cue; maybe sounds above human hearing, or perhaps electrical or magnetic signals, he thought. For the next three years Fabre tried to find out what it was that so attracted the males. Using peacock emperors, oak beauties, and some other moths, he finally plumped for smell, for only when he isolated the female inside a *sealed* bell-jar did the moth invasion cease. If he released strong-smelling sulphurous compounds into the room, though, the males were unaffected.

Then he noticed that the male moths had great plumed antennae. If he snipped them off, the male was unable to locate the caged female. From his observations he proposed that the female releases a scent which is attractive to the male, but he could only explain away the direction-finding ability of the male with the belief that unknown radiations, something like olfactory X-rays or smell vibrations which could spread enormous distances, were given off by the female.

Other European naturalists had been equally intrigued. Earlier, in the eighteenth century, René Antoine Ferchault de Reaumur, F. Ch. Lesser, and August Johann Rosel von Rosenhof wrote about male moths being attracted to virgin females. Rudolph Mell, from Germany, made small identifiable nicks in the wings of male silk moths and released them from railway stations progressively further away from his home.

Marked individuals would return to a caged female from up to 4.5 kilometres away. August Forel, the Swiss pyschiatrist and entomologist, placed a female moth on some paper then hung the paper alone out of the window. Sure enough, the males arrived in huge numbers, and to sexologist Forel's consternation, and to the amusement of Lausanne's *Gassenbuben* or street urchins gathered on the pavement below, the moths tried to mate with the paper. Vibrations from the female were definitely not involved, thought Forel, which brought the focus back to an olfactory sense.

It was not until 1959, when techniques in chemistry, histology, and physiology were sufficiently advanced, that the active ingredient in the female moths' scent was isolated. Adolf Butenandt, of the Max Planck Institute, recognised the compound *trans*-10-cis-12-hexadecadien-1-ol, otherwise known as bombykol, in the scent glands of the domesticated silk moth *Bombyx mori*. The amounts of the compound involved were so minute that in order to obtain just 12 milligrams, Butenandt needed the glands of half a million moths.

Peter Karlson and Martin Lüscher, in an article in *Nature* gave the world a new word – pheromone: a new term for a class of biologically active substances. Pheromones, they said, are chemical messengers that an animal releases into the environment to influence the physiology or behaviour of another individual of the same species. Translated from the Greek, the word means 'to transfer excitement'. Further work served to separate pheromones into two groups – those that influence immediate behaviour became the 'releaser' or 'signalling pheromones', and those that effected long-term physiological changes, the 'primer pheromones'. Fabre's moths, it seems, were transferring excitement from females to males, the moth's releaser pheromone acting as a species identification signal, a stimulant, and a sexual attractant. Subsequent detailed work has revealed the way it all works.

The female moth raises her abdomen, protrudes a pair of glands from the body, releases the pheromone, flutters her wings, and wafts the scent into the air. The wind does the rest. A plume of pheromone spreads down wind from the female and can be considerably diluted by the time it is found by a passing male. The male, however, can detect just one molecule, if it should land on his antennae.

At the Max Planck Institute, Deitrich Schneider and his colleagues have been examining the way that the male silk moth's feathery antennae pick up the pheromone. Along the branches of the antennae are the receptor organs, each consisting of a hollow hair containing two nerve endings bathed in a fluid. The pheromone molecules are thought to enter the sensory hairs via pores on its surface, pass down a tubule, and make contact with a pheromone receptor cell. Changes in the electrical condition of the surface of the receptor cell activate the nerves and the nerve impulse winds its way into the insect's nervous system. Because of continuous accidental background firing of the receptor cells, about 200 molecules of pheromone are required before the male moth changes direction. Of the 60,000 sensory hairs on the antennae of male moths nearly three-quarters are tuned specifically to respond to the female's pheromone.

On receipt of sufficient stimulus the male turns to face the wind, flies upwind against the air current and then, by a series of zigzags, flies up a gradient to the source of the smells. How, though, does a male find and follow the olfactory plume of one particular female, when there may be many releasing pheromones at the same time? It has been found that most moths fly at the same time each evening, and so the amount of 'cross-talk' is likely to be further enhanced, and confusing. At Cornell University, William Conner and his colleagues think they may have an answer. They discovered that the release of the pheromone by the female is not a continuous and passive secretion, but is carried out in short bursts. The pheromone is puffed out by the bella moth *Utetheisa ornatrix* at a rate of 1.5 pulses per second. This would give a male moth that little extra directional information to enable him to home in on a female.

Another problem is the swamping of the signal as the male picks up more and more pheromone when he gets closer and closer to the female. Why don't the male's antennae become desensitised? At the University of Washington in Seattle, Richard Vogt and Lynn Riddiford, working with the wild silk moth *Antheraea polyphemus*, have identified proteins produced on the antennae of the male that interact with the pheromone of the female, and cancel the signal in two stages. There is a rapid first step of de-activation followed by slower enzyme degradation. The rapid clearing is important for the zigzag flight, for the moth is finding its direction by sampling air for pheromone molecules both inside and outside the chemical plume from the female. The moth must be aware immediately when it has left the plume. The second step is important to remove pheromones from the antennae receptors, or they would simply clog-up.

In some species it has been found that the concentration of the scents is critical. Although males respond to very low dilutions, too much, it seems, is not a turn on.

Temperature can be important too. Most moths do not release sex pheromones when the temperature is below 16°C, but the North American winter moth *Operophtera brumata* prefers 7 to 15°C, thereby extending its sexual activities well into late autumn.

When a male moth is in close proximity to the female he begins the 'whirring dance', for he must now court her and persuade her to mate. Male silk moths circle the female, beating their wings furiously, and every so often diving down and brushing against the female's antennae. He is dusting her with his own pheromone. One function of this behaviour seems to be the inhibition of the female's flight reaction.

Studies of the queen butterfly *Danaus gilippus berenice*, by Tom Eisner and Thomas Pliske, at Cornell, have shown the importance of the male's chemical courtship. As day-fliers, the male queen butterflies are able to find their mate by sight rather than by chemicals, but their antics when close to the female serve to illustrate the general principles of courtship. In this case the male overtakes the female in flight and brushes his abdomen against her antennae. He will flutter about in front of her for some time before they settle down. Closer examination revealed that the male has a pair of extrudable brush-like 'hair-pencils', that are tucked away most of the time, but are extended during courtship. The male brushes the 'hair-pencil' against the female's antennae and head leaving behind minute spherules of cuticle, which adhere to the female's body by means of a sticky coating. Removal of the 'hair-pencils' meant that the males could court but did not mate. Contained within the 'dust' is an aphrodisiac which the female must receive before the four to five hours' actual mating session can take place.

One curiosity not resolved is that male queen butterflies have wing pouches into which they place their 'hair-pencils' several times a day. What role the pouches play is not known, for their removal does not seem to affect the onset of mating.

In the courtship of grayling butterflies *Hipparchia* spp., studied by Niko Tinbergen, the female settles on the ground, and the male flies down and walks in front of her. At first he carries out a visual display of wing opening and closing, showing off his eye-spots and colour bands, but then traps the female's antennae between his wings. Scales on the forewing, coated with pheromone, are transferred to the female and appear to stimulate her to accept him for mating.

Two species of Asian arctiid moths, *Creatonotos* spp., extrude four enormous hair-covered tubes, like gangling brittle-star arms, from the tip of the abdomen when in the presence of a 'calling' female. Chemical examination of the arms revealed that they contain defence substances acquired from plants on which the larval stages had fed, and which had been retained through the pupal stage and into the adult. The plant materials are thought to be utilised by the male *Creatonotos* as a sex phero-mone.

Chemical attraction has been taken to an extreme in one species of vapourer moth, *Orgyia splendida*, for the female not only has become totally flightless, but also never leaves the con-fines of the cocoon. Sex pheromones serve to entice the male. He flies down and smears his own scent, and the female makes a hole in the pupal case to give him access for mating. The eggs are then laid in the cocoon, and the female dies beside her new brood.

Pheromones, isolated and chemically analysed, from the gypsy moth *Lymantria dispar* have been synthesised and used for con-trolling this pest species. Gyplure, as the substance is known, is released into the wild in order to contact the males before they can reach the females. Thus, males and females are kept apart and unable to reproduce. Similar control operations have been carried out with other pest species of moths, where the optimum period of mating activity has been recognised, and the spraying of synthetic pheromones confined to fixed periods, reducing the amount of material needed and the degree of disturbance to the rest of the ecosystem. In North America the US Department of Agriculture confused the cotton ballworm and the tobacco budworm to such an extent that they tried to mate inter-specifically, and the resulting mismatch meant that the moths became inextricably locked together, only to die in each other's legs.

The female Australian bola spider *Dicrostichus magnificus* has taken advantage of the sex pheromone system of the moths to obtain her food. She dangles a sticky bolus, coated with the pheromone normally released by virgin female moths, to entice and entrap eager males. The wing fluttering of the would-be suitors triggers the spider to flick the bolus and, according to Mark Stowe, of Harvard University, a spider has been seen to catch as many as eight moths in a night. When a moth is trapped, the sticky globule is hauled in for the feast, although it can stretch if necessary to absorb the energy of a particularly large, struggling moth.

Spiders themselves, like many other groups of animals, produce sex pheromones during courtship and mating. There is often great reluctance on the part of the male spider to approach the female in case he gets eaten up. Female web spiders encourage their prospective mates to overcome their apprehensions by secreting into the threads of the web sex pheromone. This serves to release the male's courtship behaviour, and also attracts him to mate.

Similarly, male spiders of the genus *Pardosa* follow a pheromone-impregnated thread on the ground to locate the female.

Honey-bee queens, on the nuptial flight, release an aerial pheromone trail which the attendant drones must follow. Bumble-bee drones lay down scent trails by daubing olfactory signposts around a regular flight circuit. When a female intercepts the pheromone circuit she hangs abot in wait for the male on his next time round.

In some millepedes and cockroaches the males evert their sexual scent glands in the presence of the female. She comes to feed on the secretions, which serve to inhibit her escape reaction and leave her immobile for mating.

The male hermit crab *Pagurus bernhardus* receives a dose of pheromone on contact with the exoskeleton of a female. This encourages him to grasp the edge of the female's shell and drag her about, sometimes for several days, until she is ready to mate.

Male American lobsters *Homarus americanus* wait in their rock crevices for a female to call by. She approaches the entrance to the crevice and squirts in a pheromone. The male responds quickly and allows her to enter. She moults her exoskeleton, and must be impregnated by the male before the new skeleton begins to harden. She is allowed, by the male, to remain in the crevice until the hardening process is complete.

Male gobiid fishes *Bathygobius soporator* approach the female and exhibit their courtship coloration and movements, such as rapid fanning, in response to the female's release of pheromones.

Male tortoises *Geochelone* spp. are sparked off by pheromones to such an extent that even a plant over which a female has crawled may be on the receiving end of the male's amorous attentions.

Mammals have been shown to have pheromones involved in

mate attraction. Male rats, for instance, tell whether a female is receptive by her smell, as do cats and dogs, as any pet-owner would verify. Rhesus macaques *Macacus mulatta* are known to produce a sexually attractive chemical at the time of ovulation that leads to mounting behaviour on the part of the males.

## Maintaining social harmony

Social insects like bees, wasps, ants and termites, mediate their lives with pheromones. The omnipotent presence of the queen, for instance, percolates to every corner of the colony. Queen substance, as it is known, prevents other members of the nest from becoming sexually mature. It is a primer pheromone that inhibits ovarian development in young virgin queens and workers, and is directly responsible in setting up and maintaining the caste system. It can be distributed in the hive by worker-to-worker contact, as an airborne chemical, in the food, or in faeces.

In the honey-bee *Apis mellifera*, queen substance has been identified as 9-oxo-2-decenoic acid. Outside the hive it serves to attract the drones during the nuptial mating flight, and at the time of swarming is used to keep the workers close to the queen. Inside, however, it strongly influences the behaviour and physiology of the worker bees. It is produced, together with several other pheromones, in the queen's mandibular gland. It is one of many communication substances produced from various parts of the queen's body, but is thought to be one of the most important in the maintenance of the colony's social structure.

When a nest is set up the queen gathers about her several worker bees that constitute the 'court'. Members of the court change regularly, individuals staying close to the queen for just a few seconds or sometimes up to half-an-hour. They are strongly attracted to the queen, and stroke her and lick her, seemingly interested in the queen substance that she produces. It is most likely that these 'messenger' bees, besides attending and grooming the queen, transfer the queen substance to the rest of the hive when they come into contact with other workers. It appears to inhibit ovary development in workers and prevent the production of new queens.

As a colony enlarges, the queen substance becomes gradually more dilute, until the point is reached when the queen's influence on the hive is considerably reduced, and the production of new queens begins. Until then, the female larvae, in their standard hexagonal cells, have received an initial feed of a nutritious substance produced from the salivary glands of the attendant workers, followed by honey and pollen. Larvae fed in this way become workers. Prospective queens, however, are placed into larger royal cells and fed the more nutritious food, known as royal jelly, throughout their development.

There is only room for one queen in the hive and so, before the new queen can emerge, the old queen must leave with her swarm. This is co-ordinated by sound. The old queen makes a 'piping' sound to which the unhatched queens reply by 'quacking'. When the piping stops it indicates that the old queen has left and the new queen can emerge to take over the colony. Her first task is to kill all her sisters.

In a termite colony, chemical control by the king and queen can be very complicated. Basically, a population of juvenile workers is maintained that can develop, as and when necessary, into an appropriate caste. If there are not enough soldiers in the colony the juveniles develop into soldiers; if something happens to the king or queen then they are brought up as replacement reproductives. If there are too many soldiers in a colony, some are killed by the juvenile workers. If the king and queen are still present in the colony, replacement reproductives are destroyed and any further development of reproductives is inhibited by regal pheromones. The pheromone is transferred from individual to individual in the faeces.

In the red fire ant *Solenopsis invicta* virgin females, although sexually mature, are prevented from shedding their wings and developing into egg-layers by a primer pheromone from the queen that is carried about the colony by the workers.

An alarm pheromone is released by honey-bees under attack. It serves to muster other bees to the battle, and a large swarm forms which is more likely to be able to deal with the attacker. Similar alarm substances are given off by termites and ants. Another fire ant *S. saevissima*, when threatened, produces an alarm chemical from its head end, and a trail of chemical from its Dufour's gland in the abdomen. The alarm warns others that danger is nearby, while the trail substance guides others to the spot where they can put up a united front.

Honey-bees use a signalling pheromone to find each other. A chemical, produced from the Nasonov gland, is discharged into a groove in the abdomen and is exposed when the abdomen is flexed. Bees that were temporarily lost, or have found new food sources, disperse the pheromone at the entrance to the hive, thus providing a chemical signpost for other bees to find the hive entrance.

When individuals from a swarm settle at a suitable homesite the Nasonov pheromone serves to attract the queen and the rest of the swarm down to rest. Researchers are attempting to synthesise the pheromone in order to encourage swarming bees to fly down and enter empty hives.

The Brazilian social wasp *Polybia sericea* might find it necessary to move house either when the colony needs to send off a reproductive swarm or when the existing nest is damaged. In the latter case, the adult wasps fly in wide circles around the nest, but gradually alight on bushes and trees nearby. Little groups form that slowly increase in numbers as wasps fly in. One group seems to dominate, probably the one containing the queen, as she is likely to be releasing a signalling pheromone, and all the other groups gather to it. When the swarm is ready to move off, a preferred direction is established and the swarm moves away.

As the swarm travels, individuals are seen to drag their abdomens on leaves and twigs along the way. It is as if they are leaving a signposted trail. And this is precisely what Robert Jeanne, of the University of Wisconsin-Madison, found to be the case. Secretions from a gland on the underside of the abdomen were being used by the wasps to mark the site of the swarm so that foragers absent at the time of the move could find the swarm again. Daubing the undergrowth with scent-markers gave foraging wasps a trail to locate the new nest site.

Several stingless bees use a similar system when recruiting workers to exploit a new food source. A *Trigona* forager, having found food, will make several journeys to and from the source and nest, scent-marking along the way with a mandibular gland secretion that provides an odour trail for other bees to follow.

African weaver ants *Oecophylla longinoda*, studied at Harvard University by Berthold Hölldobler and Edward Wilson, show a series of behaviour patterns mediated by complex chemical communication. The African weavers are small yellow ants that live in the rain-forest canopy in colonies of up to 500,000 individuals, the offspring of a single queen. The females have a three-caste system consisting of the queen, major workers and minor workers. The males play very little part in colony affairs except to be available for mating at the time of the nuptial flights. The species is characterised by its nest construction. Leaves are bonded together with a sticky silk squeezed from the developing larvae almost like toothpaste from a tube. A single weaver ant colony can occupy an entire tree.

The major caste attends to the queen. Individuals from the crowded retinue feed her with regurgitated liquid food once a minute. Occasionally a major worker lays a sterile egg which is also fed to the queen. With this constant flow of nutrients, she can lay hundreds of eggs every day. Majors also carry out all the foraging and nest-construction work. They patrol the colony repelling intruders and gathering sugar-producing bugs for their honeydew. They have, it seems, total control of their immediate environment, and this is only achieved by sophisticated communication. For example, there are five recruitment systems.

As a colony grows, so the search is started for new territory. If a good site is just out of reach, workers will clamber on top of each other to form a bridge over which more explorers can pass. To secure the new territory, the first explorers return to the main colony and recruit more workers. The route is marked with an unusually produced pheromone. The rectal gland, just inside the anal opening, is extruded and rubbed along the ground supported on a sledge-like structure formed by two stiff hairs. On finding a nest-mate the returning explorer pummels her antennae and the new recruit starts off along the odour trail towards the new territories. The pioneers stimulate others to move house by carrying off larvae and other individuals, such as minor caste workers, to the new nests.

If a new food source is encountered, the explorer similarly lays an odour trail, encourages nest-mates to take an interest by pummelling their antennae, and offers samples of the new food by regurgitating it to the recruits.

When under attack, weaver ants respond aggressively, particularly to colonies of neighbouring weaver ants. Often a no-go strip is left between two ant territories. If neighbouring ants meet, however, each ant begins a ritualised battle-dance, raising itself on to extended legs, and circling the opponent. In swashbuckling style the combatants thrust and parry with their mandibles until one is pinned to the ground. The legs and antennae are snipped off, and the abdomen cut open. Meanwhile, some workers have returned to the nest for help, leaving a rectal gland odour trail to the 'front line'. When they find nest-mates, the scouts indicate, by execution of the ritual battle-dance, but without the aggressive follow-up, that more recruits are needed for the fight. The new recruits head for the fray.

If a worker encounters an enemy but does not engage in battle, it will run about in a pattern of short loops, dragging its abdomen over the ground and spasmodically raising it into the air. On this occasion another gland, the sternal gland, is exposed and the secretion has been found to attract ants from as far away as 10 centimetres. Homing-in on the scent, recruits gather in small groups. John Bradshaw, at the University of Southampton, found that an alarm pheromone, produced from mandibular glands, further serves to draw recruits to the action. Small bands of ants can deal with quite large aggressors. Weaver ants also seem to be more confident when fighting on their own territory, which is marked by the deposition of faecal pellets.

Until now, examples of chemical manipulation by a central queen have been restricted to the terrestrial invertebrates, in particular, the social insects, but a remarkable discovery in Kenya by Jennifer Jarvis, of the University of Cape Town, has added a mammal to the list – the naked mole rat *Heterocephalus glaber*. The creature is neither a mole nor a rat, but is a class of rodent that is completely hairless. It looks like an 8-centimetre-long wrinkled sausage with enormous teeth on one end. Apart from its unusual appearance, the most bizarre aspect of its life is its social structure.

Naked mole rats live in underground colonies consisting of extensive networks of tunnels that converge on a central nesting-chamber. The colony is dominated by a 'queen', the sole breeder who is slightly larger than the rest, and 'workers' that carry out nest-building, food-carrying, refuse collection and tunnel-digging. The caste system, according to Richard Alexander of the University of Michigan, 'is one of the mammal finds of the century'. Another mole rat researcher, Paul Sherman, of Cornell University, described the species as 'the most insect-like mammals' he had ever seen. It appears that the queen retains her control over the colony by walking over and around her subjects liberally distributing pheromones. She is served by two dominant males and attended by a collection of nursemaids that look after the four litters a year. A litter usually contains ten pups. The rest of the females in a colony are not sterile, but the surrendering of the right to breed does not, for some unknown and inexplicable reason, cause any kind of social unrest. The colonies are re-markably peaceful.

The digging of tunnels is a co-operative activity. The leading mole rate finds its way along the tunnel by its whiskers. A trail of individuals behind locates the leader, probably by smell. With sharp chisel teeth the leader scrapes away the wall, about 30 centimetres below the ground, and pushes the earth between its legs to the one behind. The Number two shovels up the pile and transports it to the tunnel entrance where it is thrown out by mole rat Number three. In this way they build, co-operatively, an enormous complex of tunnels. About eighty individuals might live in the colony.

## Primordial sex

At some stage in the earth's distant past, free-living, single-celled organisms exchanging genetic material gained an advantage over those that did not. Sexual reproduction emerged, and the individual cells would have found each other more easily with the help of chemical messages. Small groups of cells, attracted to others by chemicals, eventually stayed together, some cells specialising for particular tasks, and gradually the multi-cellular organisms were formed.

Although this is a very simplistic description, it is intriguing to find that some of these events can be seen today in an organism that spends most of its life as widely dispersed single cells, but which comes together at the time of reproduction – the slime mould.

The slime mould *Dictyostelium discoideum* lives in moist soil as free-living, single-celled, amoeba-like organisms that feed on bacteria. When the food supply begins to dry up, certain individual amoebae secrete pulses of cyclic-3-'5'-adenosine monophosphate, a pheromone that serves to attract other amoebae. As they aggregate, the new arrivals begin to produce the chemical, and more and more organisms join the group. Gradually, the cells show some degree of specialisation and a multi-cellular organism is formed, consisting of a basal section, a stalk that emerges above the soil, and a fruiting body at the top. Spores from the aerial part are distributed to more favourable areas and the emerging single-celled organisms once more revert to the free-living amoeba-like feeding phase.

A spacing pheromone is released to ensure an even distribution of individuals in the new feeding environment.

Interestingly, John Tyler Bonner, of Princeton University who has carried out most of the work on slime moulds, found that the concentration of the fruiting body is achieved by a balance of the spacing and aggregating pheromones.

## It's me and I live here

An airborne pheromone is likely to be quickly dissipated and therefore relatively short-lived as a useful signal. A more permanent way of indicating identity or possession of territory is scent-marking. Chemical marking also allows an animal to pass a signal to another of the same species without having to stay around to deliver it.

Honey-bees scent-mark the entrance to hives and food sources. Bumble-bees have their circuit of scents. Weaver ants have faecal spots to identify territorial preserves. But perhaps the best studied scent-markers are the mammals.

Most people will have seen domestic dogs marking their regular paths with urine. Wolves and wild dogs do the same. The territory of a pack of North American timber wolves is indicated by a boundary line of urine marks. The high frequency with which urination occurs is often an indication that scent-marking is being carried out. The same is true of defaecation. One rabbit will, for example, deposit 800 droppings a day as a territorial marker. Male mice add a pheromone to their urine which serves to deter visiting males from the resident's territory. It also seems to reduce the aggressive tendencies of the intruder to the extent that the resident will have the upper hand in any confrontation.

The hippopotamus, with its whirling, muck-spreading tail, liberally distributes dung about its territory, while the black rhinoceros creates dung piles at points along well-worn trails in its home range. The scent is further spread about when the rhino tramples the dung pile and takes the smell on the soles of its feet along the path, a signpost for other rhinos to follow the trail. Some of the lorises, lemurs and New World monkeys carry out a similar activity by urinating on their feet and spreading the chemical signal over the trees through which they travel.

The dwarf mongoose *Helogale undulata rufula* stands on its head to reach the highest places on the bushes in order to deposit secretions from its anal glands. Hamsters and gerbils rub their flanks or undersides on rocks and logs, while rodents often rub their flanks on the walls of their tunnels.

One of the more interesting scent-markers is the oribi *Ourebia ourebia*. The adult males bite off the tall flower stems of grasses, and rub them with secretions from the antorbital gland in front of the eye. When a previously daubed stem is encountered, the oribi bites off the top and reapplies his own scent.

## A social taboo

It is perhaps interesting to muse briefly on our own olfactory abilities. Having learned about the amazing chemical communication and defence systems possessed by insects it is often the case that scientists deride the sensitivity of the human nose.

After all, we are told by researchers from Yale University that we can only discriminate from between six to twenty-two distinct smells, and even to recognise some of those we need to name them. If we do not know the name of what we are smelling we are quite likely to think it is something else. In tests, some people identified machine oil as cheese, for instance. Trained perfumiers, on the other hand, can identify 10,000 odours.

But there is more to the human nose than meets the human eye. Richard Potter, a psychologist from Vanderbilt University in Nashville, has found that children can identify their brothers' or sisters' T-shirts by their smell, and that mothers can pick out their babies by smell alone a couple of days after the infant is born.

In another study, female American college students sharing dormitories or student flats found that their menstrual cycles became synchronised. It was thought that a pheromone in sweat was the hidden factor that kept the cycles in step.

The idea that a subtle chemical communication system exists between humans is not new. In days gone by ardent suitors would attempt to win a maiden's favour by 'priming' a handkerchief under the armpit, and then waving it in front of her face, or using it to mop her brow.

George Dodds, of the University of Warwick, isolated a musk secretion from male human armpits, the owners of which were sexually excited. Synthesis of the substance, and its incorporation in after-shave preparations and body-splashes has meant a reprieve for the musk deer, from which these substances had previously been obtained.

In the Middle East an arranged marriage might fall through if an intermediary setting up the ceremony is put off by the woman's odour.

And if that all sounds a bit far-fetched, in the United States the research department of a flavours and fragrances manufacturer has come up with aerosal cans that dispense aromas designed to make people buy impulsively. There is a new car smell for second-hand car dealers and a fresh-baked bread smell for sandwich shops. It is not such a daft idea, for when you think about it we do have predictable reactions to certain smells. Rotting rubbish tends to revolt us, whereas the soothing scent of a pine forest relaxes us. Again, it is not new. The ancient Egyptians are thought to have used the aroma of sandalwood as a relaxant. Robert Henkin, director of the Centre for Molecular Nutrition and Sensory Disorders at Georgetown University

Medical School, Washington DC sees aromas being used to manipulate human behaviour and maybe treat mental disorders. Imagine the scene: at the end of a tiring day a burst of essence of sandalwood is pumped through the air-conditioning system, or sprayed from a time-release capsule around your neck, or simply squirted from an aerosol can kept in your drawer, and you can be relaxed and ready for your fight through the evening rush-hour traffic.

On the other hand, is this not something that could be abused – a new form of chemical warfare where entire populations could be controlled by odours? Lacewings, bees and ants do it, so why not humans? The mind, or perhaps I should say the nose, boggles.

# Sensory Worlds

Man cannot, without the help of the right technology, see ultra-violet and infra-red light, nor hear ultrasounds or infra-sounds. Apart from putting our heads on the railway track to hear the train coming, or against the ground to hear distant horses, we are relatively insensitive to vibrations. And, despite an actor's performance being described as electrifying, we make little use of an electrical field produced naturally around the body for communication or defence. With the development of the right detectors, though, we have come to appreciate that other creatures *do* make use of these forces, and in doing so, often exploit them to the extreme.

## Through the eye of a bee
In 1800 the astronomer Sir William Herschel placed a thermometer in the various parts of the sun's spectrum to see if there were any detectable temperature differences between the colours. He found the highest temperature coming from a colourless band at the red end. A year later the German physicist Johann Ritter was experimenting with the way that silver chloride broke down in the presence of light (the basis of black-and-white photography) and found that the portion of the spectrum which did this most efficiently was an invisible band beyond violet. Later these bands of light, invisible to the naked eye, became known as the infra-red and the ultraviolet. Gradually, naturalists too became aware of these two bands of light with the realisation that many creatures can detect and use them in their everyday lives.

Karl von Frisch conditioned bees to associate sources of food with particular colours. A watch-glass containing a sugar solution was placed on a coloured square in a chequer-board of squares of different colours. Empty watch-glasses were placed on the other squares. The bees went unerringly to the sugar solution. This was repeated several times in order to condition the insects to the chosen square. After a while von Frisch took away the sugar solution and replaced it with an empty watch-glass. The bees still came to that particular square. After many tests with different-coloured squares he was able to conclude that bees are sensitive to colours, but are unable to distinguish between, red, black and dark grey. Brightness differences were eliminated as cues, and later work confirmed von Frisch's initial findings that honey-bees are able to see in the ultraviolet part of the spectrum that is invisible to the human eye. They are blind, however, to the red end of the visual spectrum. Since von Frisch's experiments with honey-bees, many other creatures have been found to see in ultraviolet light, and the ultraviolet world is one we are only just beginning to be able to see our-selves.

New photographic and video techniques have allowed re-searchers to take a peek at objects reflecting ultraviolet light. Equipped with special lenses and filters, Tom Eisner's Cornell contingent have discovered that many features in the natural world look quite different when seen through the eye of a bee.

'To the uninitiated', wrote Eisner, 'the first ultraviolet view of a meadow in mixed bloom is unforgettable. Evenly tinted flowers, which to the naked eye appear to lack the usual central or radial colour-markings that direct an alighted pollinator to its goal, are suddenly revealed to possess such markings in the ultraviolet.'

What seemed to be plain yellow petals on the flowers of the black-eyed Susan, for instance, turned out to be patterned in ultraviolet light. At the base of each petal is an ultraviolet ab-sorption zone, invisible to us, but clearly seen by the bee. This nectar guide is thought to help pollinating insects not only to find the nectar glands, but also to direct them into the best position to pick up pollen. It works much like the runway landing lights at a large airport. The Cornell researchers went on to find that the absorption zone in black-eyed Susan flowers contains three chemicals of a group known as flavonol glucosides, compounds that are common in flower petals, and for which no function was known. It is suggested that they are used by plants specifically for the visual attraction of insect pollinators, and they comple-ment the acanthocyanins and carotenoids in providing flower coloration.

Closer examination of the meadow revealed that flowers with visible patterns are even more adorned when seen in ultraviolet rays. Clumps of composites, seemingly in competition for the attention of pollinators, can be distinguished quite easily by the insects. Likewise, young flowers or buds not ready for pollination often lack the ultraviolet patterns of the mature flowers on the same plant.

One curiosity that caught Eisner's ultraviolet eye was that animals that appear to be well camouflaged are actually quite conspicuous. The crab spider, for instance, sits well disguised in flower-heads waiting for prey to be attracted to the flower. To our eyes it is almost invisible, being the same colour as the flower and even having some of the same patterning as the stamens. In ultraviolet light, and to its prospective prey, however, it is very conspicuous. Why this should be, we have no idea.

Some male and female butterflies appear identical to the un-aided human eye, but in ultraviolet light they are revealed to be quite different. The pieridiid butterfly *Eroessa chilensis*, for example, is black and white, with orange patches on the fore-wings. The male and female look the same to us, but not to other *Eroessa* butterflies, for they are actually dimorphic. Only the male reflects ultraviolet light from the orange wing patches. Other butterflies, like male pierids, show a brilliant ultraviolet flicker when in flight. It seems as if Eisner and his colleagues are getting a tantalising glimpse of a whole new signalling system and 'language' that insects use in their private sensory domains.

It is tempting to speculate that the evolution of ultraviolet-absorption nectar guides in flowers has paralleled the evolution in insects of ultraviolet vision and of mouth-parts designed to extract nectar from flowers – to the benefit of both parties. If this is the case, flowers pollinated and exploited by nectar-feeding birds and bats are not likely to have ultraviolet nectar guides. Eisner examined several species of flowers from the family Gesneriaceae and found this to be the case.

But, in 1980, Timothy Goldsmith, of Yale University, revealed that three species of humming-birds – the black-chinned *Archilochus alexandri*, the blue-throated *Lampornis clemenciae*, and the magnificent or Rivoli's *Eugenes fulgens* – were able to dis-tinguish near ultraviolet light. This ability was attributed to the presence of oil droplets in the cones in the retina of the birds' eyes (a feature of the retina of birds and reptiles but not of mammals) and was responsible for the correction of focusing problems which would normally be associated with ultraviolet wavelengths. In the absence of these droplets, the human eye, and the eyes of most other placental mammals, cut off at blue wavelengths to avoid the defect known as chromatic aberration. Other vertebrates, such as toads, newts and lizards have been shown to detect ultraviolet light, as have chickens and pigeons.

As for the absence of nectar guides in flower species frequented by humming-birds and bats, it might be that there has not been enough 'evolutionary time or pressure' for them to be developed. But then, only a limited number of plants have been examined. Nevertheless, the discovery that avian species can see at the ultraviolet end of the spectrum has other evolutionary implications.

The loss of the oil droplets in the mammalian eye may have been an adaptation to an earlier nocturnal way of life, maybe at the time the primitive mammals were emerging in the shadow of the more dominant reptile species. Although many mammals have now adopted a diurnal lifestyle, the oil droplet system has been lost forever, and today the human eye is, in a way, making the best of a bad job. It is likely that the eye of the bird is closer to the ideal diurnal eye, and that this revelation may lead us to discover unsuspected visual capacities in many other animals. In his paper in the American journal *Science*, Goldsmith summarised it as follows: '. . . the interplay of several spectral classes of oil droplets with several cone pigments, and the presence of receptors functioning in the near UV suggest that avian colour vision possesses a richness that lies beyond our ken'.

## Hearing the unheard

In 1880 Pierre Curie, husband of Marie Curie and co-discoverer of radium, uncovered a property of certain asymetric crystals (like quartz) that causes them to vibrate when subjected to a rapidly changing electrical potential, or to produce a positive and negative charge on opposite faces when subjected to pressure. It is known as the 'piezo-electric effect', and is the principle on which microphones and record players were developed. When a slither of quartz is hooked up to an electric current at a frequency that equals the natural vibration of the mineral, it produces very high frequency waves, known as ultrasound.

In 1912 the *Titanic* hit an iceberg and Louis Richardson was prompted to suggest 'supersonic' sound echoes as a way of finding submerged objects. In 1916 the French physicist Paul Langevin successfully transmitted ultrasonic waves about 3 kilometres underwater, and bounced them off an iron plate placed 100 metres away. A Royal Navy team, under the direction of Professor R. W. Boyle, was ready, in 1918, with a viable underwater detection system, known as ASDIC (Allied Submarine Detection Investigation Committee), a name to be superseded by the American acronym, SONAR (Sound Navigation and Ranging). Then, in 1938, Professor G. W. Pierce and his graduate student at Harvard, Donald Griffin, revealed that bats had the ability to emit and detect ultra-high frequency sounds, and that they were using these sounds to orientate and navigate by echo location. Bats, they had found, had developed ultrasonic echo location many millions of years before man discovered it.

To be fair, Lazzaro Spallanzini came close to working it out in 1793. He discovered that bats could fly normally, and detect and avoid obstacles in flight, even when their eyes were covered or removed. His experiments were very cruel. He would blind bats and block their ears with all sorts of substances. One wonders how a naturalist with such a fascination with animals could treat them with such contempt. Nevertheless, Spallanzini eliminated taste, touch, smell and vision as the senses involved in bat navigation. If he covered the ears, however, blinded bats could not fly properly and would collide with obstacles and walls. Whatever sense was being used, it involved the ears, but Spallanzani could hear no sounds.

Louis Jurine, one of Spallanzini's colleagues in Geneva also proposed sound, and Spallanzini himself suggested that reflected sound was involved in object perception. In 1826 Sir Anthony Carlisle in England recognised 'extreme acuteness of hearing, as the Bat, when its ears were covered, flew against obstacles as if unconscious of their presence'. Spallanzini and Jurine considered low-frequency sounds from wingbeats and body movements as a likely sound source. The French anatomist, Georges Cuvier, had already proposed touch as the most likely explanation, and this was further supported by the German, J. Schöbl, in 1871 and by A. Whitaker in 1906. Two years later, in the USA, W. L Hahn repeated many of Spallanzini's experiments and found that when plaster of Paris was placed in bats' ears they could no longer avoid obstacles in the dark. He proposed a 'sixth sense'. Sir Hiram Maxim, another scientist prompted by the sinking of the *Titanic*, in 1912, examined 'the sixth sense' hypothesis as a means of detecting obstacles from the bows of ships. But in 1920 Hamilton Hartridge, at Cambridge University, wrote a paper on 'The Avoidance of Objects by Bats in their Flight' and suggested '. . . that they possess some sense, the homologue of which is not possessed by man'. His conclusions were based on Langevin and Boyle's work on underwater submarine detection systems, and he proposed '. . . that bats during flight emit a short wavelength note and that this sound is reflected from objects in the vicinity. The reflected sound gives the bat information concerning its surroundings. If the path ahead is clear of obstacles, no sound waves are reflected back to the listener. If there are obstacles, then these will reflect the sound and the bat will receive an audible warning.' By 1938 G. W. Pierce had invented the apparatus to confirm Hartridge's hypothesis and Don Griffin carried out his classic experiments. Today we know that man is unusual in the animal kingdom in not being able to appreciate very high frequencies, for research has shown that many groups of animals communicate, orient or navigate using ultrasound.

Even before the bat discoveries, Pierce had used his 'supersonic' sound-detector to record the ultrasonic courtship songs of bush-crickets, which he wrote about in his book, *The Songs of Insects*, published in 1948.

In the 1950s Kenneth Roeder and Asher Treat of Tufts University discovered that noctuiid moths could detect the ultrasonic cries of bats that were chasing them, and David Pye, at Queen Mary College, London, went on to show that they could take avoiding action by jamming the bat sonar with ultrasonics of their own. At about the same time John Anderson, of Cornell University, found that laboratory rats and mice emitted ultrasounds. In the 1960s, Ellian Noirot, revealed that baby mice communicate with the mother by means of ultrasonic calls, which led Gillian Sales, at King's College, London, to find a whole ultrasonic vocabulary in a variety of rodents, including aggression and submission calls between adult male rats, courtship calls in golden hamsters and distress calls in field mice. (For a more detailed account of bat sonar and other ultrasonic communications systems see *Animal Language*, BBC, 1984.)

For me, though, the most intriguing ultrasound users are the whales and dolphins and, in particular, the theory that they may be producing very high levels of ultrasound in order to stun, and perhaps kill, prey.

## Killing with sound

It has long puzzled marine biologists how an enormous creature the size of a double-decker bus – the sperm whale – can chase and catch the streamlined, jet-powered giant squid. But catch them it does; witness the remains of gigantic 6 to 9 metre-long squid in the stomachs of sperm whales sliced open on the decks of whaling ships, and the great, saucer-shaped sucker marks along sperm whale heads, evidence of extraordinary battles in the depths of the oceans. Recent underwater film of sperm whale herds in the Indian Ocean does, in fact, reveal them to be supple and graceful swimmers, but still does not show that they have sufficient speed to run down a giant squid. The secret might be in the sperm whale's large, bulbous head.

Sperm whales are odontocetes or 'toothed' whales and are related to the dolphins and porpoises. To explain how their head has something to do with catching squid we must begin our story with their smaller relatives.

Soon after Pierce had developed his ultrasonic-detector, alert researchers began to examine many animals for signs of high-frequency sound production. Sea creatures were no exception. Winthrop Kellogg, William Schevill and Barbara Lawrence were the first to demonstrate, in 1953, that the bottle-nose dolphin *Tursiops truncatus* is able to produce and hear ultrasounds. Ken Norris, with the performing circus dolphin, Kathy, then went on to show that the ultrasounds are focused in a beam in front of the dolphin's head, and are used in echo location. The principle of echo location in dolphins had already been proposed by Arthur McBride at Marine Studios (later Marineland) in Florida. Kathy would be blindfolded, with the aid of suction cups on both eyes, and invited to swim through an obstacle course or recover objects in her tank. This she did with complete ease.

For some time emphasis shifted from the ultrasonic direction-finding abilities of dolphins to the audible communication between individuals, and the fantasy of being able to have mean-ingful discussions between man and dolphin. Other researchers examined the way that dolphins produce and receive ultrasounds.

Anatomical studies indicate that the ultrasounds are produced by structures in the modified nostril region below the blow-hole – how is still not completely clear. Air is forced backwards and forwards through the complicated plumbing system causing nasal plugs to vibrate. The sounds leave the body through the forehead, where they are focused by the 'melon', to a point about a metre in front of the head. The melon is a fatty body containing highly specialised lipids. Donald Malins, of the US National Marine Fisheries Service, together with Usha Varanasi, of Seattle University, and Henry Feldman of Washington University, have carried out a detailed analysis of the melon and have found an area of unusual lipids made of isovaleric acid, a compound rarely found in other animals. From the three-dimensional structure of the fats they have found that the melon is, indeed, a sound lens. The ultrasounds are bent by the lipid molecules into the focused beam. Evolution has apparently favoured a narrowing of the beam, for the more primitive river dolphins of the Far East have broad sound beams whereas the more advanced coastal and ocean-going dolphins have thin, pencil-beams. This narrowing of the beam has also brought with it an increase in the intensity of the sounds to a level that the dolphin could conceivably use to debilitate prey.

Whitlow Au and A. E. Murchison working in Hawaii measured the intensity of sounds produced by a bottle-nose dolphin that was undergoing long-range discrimination tests. A small sphere, about the size of a tangerine, was placed over 100 metres underwater from the dolphin. The creature was able to locate it easily and, in doing so, produced a burst of ultrasound that was so loud it was close to the finite limit of sound. Any higher and the sound would have turned to heat. It was the loudest sound ever recorded from a dolphin. Ken Norris, at the University of California at Santa Cruz, and Bertel Møhl, of Aarhus University, Denmark, speculated that the dolphin might use this intense sound beam to stun and catch prey. In the USSR, V. M. Bel'Kovitch and A. V. Yablakov calculated that dolphin echo location sound should have enough energy to affect the behaviour of prey fish. Ken Norris reasoned that if the dolphin has evolved the wherewithal for a sound beam weapon then it is likely to use it. He organised some tests to find out.

First, man-made high-intensity sound beams were found to knock out fish. Then, dolphins in captivity were presented with live fish in their tank, and the behaviour of the fish and the dolphins was closely watched. After a short while the three dolphins in the test began to spray the fish with ultrasound. The fish were rather larger than those normally taken by the dolphins so it was not expected that the dolphins would be able to kill them. For over an hour the dolphins directed sound at the fish school.

'A dolphin would make a run at the school, attempting to put the fish right on the tip of its beak,' said Norris. 'The fish school would split, head for the tail of the dolphin, and re-form. Slowly, though, the fish school became depolarised'.

Norris noticed after a while that the fish were not all facing the same direction. Individuals began to wander from the safety of the school, seemingly disoriented. Similar observations have been made in the wild. Striped dolphins *Stenella coeruleoalba* have been seen to circle an anchovy school, spray them with sound, and then cut across the school, shovelling fish into their mouths at will. The anchovies do not attempt to escape their fate.

Something has frozen them to the spot. It could, of course, be a biproduct of the initial chase. A build-up of waste materials in the blood, for instance, might disable the muscles.

Off the coast near Vancouver, where marine biologists have been studying one of the larger odontocetes, the killer whale, one observer saw a large salmon, heading for its 'home' river, stop 'dead in its tracks' only to be gobbled up by a killer whale following behind. The fish could have easily outpaced the whale, but it didn't; it simply stopped.

Two other pieces of evidence showing the production of high levels of sound come from captive dolphins. At many marine circuses and aquaria, divers entering the water to feed their charges have experienced a curious tickling sensation on the back of the neck which they attribute to the dolphins' echo location system. It is also clear that several dolphins in a tank are likely to 'hit' each other. Might there be echo location manners, thought Ken Norris?

With such a formidable weapon, it would be very easy for one dolphin, in an actively feeding school, to annoy or even damage one of its fellows. Dolphins are known to be temperamental, so any infringement of living-space is likely to trigger a violent reaction within the school. Norris watched and listened carefully to individuals in a tank and found that not once did they echo locate each other. As a dolphin crossed in front of another, the one actively echo locating would swtich off its gear, turn its head away, and then switch back on again when the way was clear.

Which brings us back to sperm whales. Could it be that these enormous creatures are capable of producing ultrasounds at high intensities like their smaller cousins, the dolphins? Malcolm Clarke, of the Marine Biological Laboratory at Plymouth, an authority on both giant squid and sperm whales, directed high-intensity beams of sound at squid and found that they succumbed. Are sperm whales doing the same?

Sperm whales are highly vocal animals and it has long been known that they can create a great deal of noise. In 1835 Thomas Beale wrote about sperm whales retaining contact over great distances; then, in 1957, L. V. Worthington and William Schevill described the underwater sounds from sperm whales; and in 1959 Hans Hass recalled diving with a harpooned whale off the Azores and hearing 'a most curious noise . . . like the creaking of a huge barn door turning on rusty hinges'.

Sperm whales live in social groups. Sound communication is an important aspect of their lives, so it is likely to be well developed. William Watkins, using an underwater microphone array, found that a sperm whale herd would be together at the surface but would dive in the shape of an inverted funnel when going after food. They fanned out but retained contact across the kilometres of ocean with sound signals, each sperm whale in the herd having its own distinct coda of clicks. In order to remain in contact in the sea, such sound signatures would have to be pretty loud, indicating that these whales are capable of high-intensity sound production.

As with the dolphins, little is known about the sound-producing structures in the sperm whale head. It is, however, an interesting head, dominated by the spermaceti organ, and equipped with an intricate plumbing system of nasal passages and air sacs, all of which are thought to be in some way involved in a variety of functions including buoyancy and sound production. The spermaceti organ itself is an enormous structure filled with oil. Below it is an area of tough spongy cells, also containing oil, and known as the junk. A nasal passage on the left side of the head connects to the blow-hole. On the right is another, narrower, nasal passage connected to a pair of lips, known as the 'museau du singe', and a couple of air sacs. Here, it is thought, is the sound-production centre.

Ken Norris, working with G. W. Harvey, suggested that the spermaceti organ, like the dolphin melon, has an acoustic function, focusing ultrasounds for long-distance communication. Chemical and physical analysis showed that spermaceti oil is a good sound conductor. At great depths it is likely that the ultrasonic clicks are also used to locate food in the inky darkness. Might they take that function a little further and stun the prey as well?

In 1963, Bel'Kovitch and Yablakov, in a paper in the Soviet journal *Yuchnyi Tekhnik* entitled 'The whale, an ultrasonic projector', proposed that the sperm whale is able to focus sound and immobilise animal prey with a sonic boom. Further support for the hypothesis came from another researcher, A. A. Berzin, who noticed that a number of sperm whales caught by whale-fishers looked as if they had congenital deformities of the lower jaw. The lower jaw was curved in such a way that the whales would have been unable to close their jaws to capture prey. Their stomachs, however, were filled with squid, and as far as could be seen the animals were otherwise perfectly healthy. Berzin concluded that the sperm whale is able to get its tonne or so of squid a day by using sound to stun them.

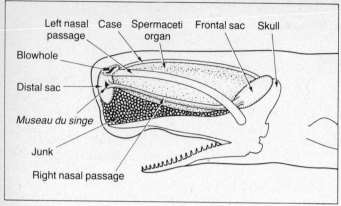

*Cross-section of head of sperm whale.*

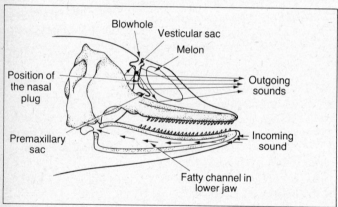

*Cross-section of head of dolphin.*

Berzin also reports on sperm whales diving down to the bottom of the sea and disturbing bottom-dwellers. Whales swim along with their mouths wide open, ploughing through the sediments and sometimes damaging undersea cables. Berzin suggests that when fish and squid are uncovered, the whale narrows its ultrasonic beam, focuses on the prey, and hits it with a sudden blast of sound which knocks it out. The whale can then scoop the fish up with comparative ease. Since sperm whales are so rare, and since studying behaviour at great depths is difficult, it is likely to be some time before these proposals can be verified.

## Sitting on the surface

Before the Battle of Trafalgar in 1805, Nelson was unable to see the combined French and Spanish fleets leaving Cadiz for they were too far over the horizon from his flagship, HMS *Victory*. The first ship in the line, however, could see the enemy ships, and a message was passed from ship to ship until it reached Nelson, and he was able to take the appropriate action.

Ocean skaters (or striders) *Halobates robustus* are marine insects that live, like naval flotillas, on the surface film of the sea off the rocky coast of the Galapagos Islands in the Pacific Ocean. Since the males are flightless and do not dive, they can be considered, for experimental purposes, to be living in a two-dimensional world. For this reason, they were the subject of a study by John Treherne and William Foster, at the University of Cambridge. They had noticed that ocean skaters, at the edge of flotillas, increased their rate of locomotion and turning in response to the arrival of a predator, such as a lava lizard (*Tropidurus* spp.) or a yellow warbler (*Dendroica* spp.), and that this activity was rapidly transmitted to the rest of the individuals in the flotilla. They called the behaviour 'the Trafalgar effect', and it is thought that the confusion caused by the random movement, and the consequent reflections of light from the skaters' bodies, would confer a degree of protection on the individuals in the flotilla. What was puzzling, however, was the way that the skaters were communicating.

Visual and tactile cues have been identified in pond skaters, the freshwater relatives of ocean skaters. They signal – to repel an advance, for instance – by raising the leg nearest to the intruder, or by extending their legs, like stilts, to scare it away. During courtship and copulation, male skaters have been seen to touch females with their antennae and then shake the antennae rapidly. But perhaps the most interesting means of communication so far discovered is the way that skaters signal to one another by producing ripples on the surface of the water.

Ripple communication has been studied in Australian pond skaters by R. Stimson Wilcox, of the State University of New York at Binghampton. The male of one species, *Rhagadotarsus kraepelini*, that lives in gently flowing streams or in ponds in the tropics from India to Australia, has been seen to make ripple signals during courtship and for spacing out individuals.

The insect produces the ripples by waving one of its pairs of legs vertically on the surface of the water. In addition, *Rhagadotarsus* grasps a signalling site, such as a small twig, from which it produces the ripples. The sites are important in court-ship and mating for this species exhibits a form of lekking behaviour. Males and females gather in assembly areas or leks to display during courtship and mating. The signalling site is also the place where the female will lay her eggs after copulation, and so several males defend territories around the site, each vying for her attention. Twenty-two waves a second will win over a female, and her ripple-discrimination is so acute she can distinguish signals 1.5 ripples per second apart, at a distance of 40–60 centi-metres from the signaller.

Wilcox has studied another pond skater in North America, *Gerris remigis*, and found that the males produce high-frequency, 85–90 waves per second, signals to warn other males to stay away. It is effective over a radius of 9–10 centimetres.

Males can also determine whether an approaching skater is a welcome female or a hostile male, for it is only the male that pro-duces the high-frequency signal. Wilcox devised an ingenious apparatus to check this. He attached minute magnets to the legs of females and then placed the individuals within an electro-magnetic field. A computer was used to generate the high-frequency signals, and each time the magnetic coil was energised the leg of the female would be moved up and down, imitating the movements normally associated with a male. A group of males were fitted with miniature blindfolds and let loose with the magnetic female and with normal females. Courtship in this species mostly takes place at night, and so the experiment was designed to mimic those conditions. The males courted and mated with the normal females but left the females generating male-style signals well alone.

One other function of ripple communication might be to identify others of the same species. This is vital, for pond skaters eat anything that moves, and have been known to be cannibalis-tic. In West Germany, Horst Lang, of the University of Karstanz, has been studying the voracious backswimmer, *Notonecta*, and has discovered that individuals can discriminate between the ripple patterns of adults and nymphs of its own species and of other potentially hostile species.

The means of detecting ripple signals has not yet been determined for pond skaters, but it is likely that stretch-receptors picking up distortions in the insect's exoskeleton, or the sensing of movements of sensory hairs is being used. Both systems are used by *Notonecta*. Either way, they are very accurate at locating a signalling source. The difference in time of a ripple hitting adjacent legs would give the information, although there is some evidence from the work of Rod Murphey, of the State University of New York at Albany, that skaters are able to gain directional information from just one leg.

These insects are also very sensitive to movements below the surface, which brings us back to *Halobates*. Apparently it is impossible for a fish, unless it has a large enough mouth to suck down a huge gulp of water, to catch an adult ocean skater.

## A shocking tail

If humans could detect naturally the electric and electromagnetic events that take place in the sea and in rivers and lakes, we would experience a whole new world – an electric environment. It is a dimension available for underwater creatures to use, and Nature, in her wisdom, has seen fit to use it. The group which seems to have taken every advantage of it is the fish. There are fish that detect small changes of electrical potentials in the water, others that produce their own current, and those that detect the geomagnetic field. Of those that produce electricity, the dangerous electric eels of the Amazon, the electric catfish of Africa, and the electric torpedo rays of the oceans are well known. They can store such a large charge that they can knock out a full-grown person. But there are other fishes that do not seem to use their electricity for defence or attack; rather, they orient, navigate and communicate using an electrical sense. They are known collectively as the 'weak-electric fishes', and their story was not uncovered until the late 1950s.

In 1958, Walter Lissman, of the University of Cambridge, found that certain freshwater fish produced very weak electric fields, and that they could find their way about in their underwater environment by detecting disturbances in the field. Since those initial observations it has been found that several fishes not only electro-locate, but also electro-communicate. It is an effective system for a fish to use – it can be turned on and off instantaneously, pass through turbid water, and travel around barriers like rocks and submerged roots. It is also surprisingly 'private', for electro-reception is not a common sense found in underwater creatures. There are going to be too few messages to jam the communication channel. The only drawback is distance. The freshwater, tube-snouted mormyrid fishes from Africa, for instance, have an effective range of 100 centimetres for electro-communication and only 10 centimetres for electro-location.

The electric current is generated by modified muscles or

nerves. An electric organ might consist of several strips of flattened cells, known as electrocytes, which can be found in various parts of the body. Most of the South American and African weak-electric fishes have modified axial and tail muscles adapted to produce electricity, although one group of neotropical fishes, the apteronotids, have modified nerves. The electric current produced can be in the form of simple discharges or complex signals. One species of gymnotid, a South American knifefish, *Hypopomus artedi* has the posterior and anterior faces of its electrocytes discharging at slightly different times, giving it a species-specific phased signal. Another knifefish, *Apteronotus* spp., which has its electrocytes derived from nerve tissue, discharges at the phenomenal rate of 1800 pulses per second, almost at the limit for electrical signalling.

Electro-location works very simply when an object, possessing conductivity that is different from the water, distorts the fish's electric field. An object with a lower conductivity, for instance, will lower the density of the fish's electric field lines nearest to the object. This is detected in the fish by electro-receptors all over the body, and registers as a reduction in the rate that the receptors are triggered. An object with a higher conductivity does the opposite. The receptors nearest the object will be affected more than the rest, and thus the fish obtains information about its location and electrical properties.

Many of the weak-electric fishes have enhanced their electrical image by developing focusing systems. The knifefishes tend to bend their tails around an object under investigation, whereas the elephant fish swim backwards and forwards, scanning the object and increasing their electric pulse-rate for more information.

Electro-communication has been found to parallel other modes of communication to the extent that 'electro-languages' have developed. Fundamental to communication is the ability to transmit information about the identity of the individual – its species, sex, stage of development and age. Also useful is motivational information such as readiness to mate, proclamation of territory, spacing signals and information about the quality of the prospective mate. Weak-electric fish, it turns out, have distinct signal patterns for many of these functions.

Scientists have identified two types of signallers – the pulse species with bursts of electrical activity at low-discharge rates, and the wave species with more continuous, high-frequency discharges, that broadcast in species-specific wavebands. Many of

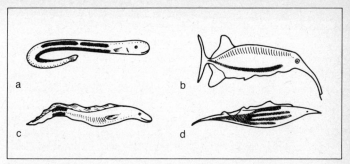

*Dark areas show arrangement of electrical organs in a) electric eel b) elephant-trunk fish c) South American knifefish d) African knifefish.*

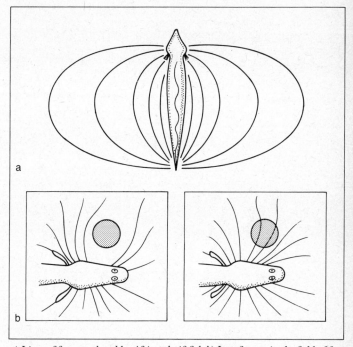

*a) Lines of force produced by African knifefish b) Interference in the field of force can be interpreted to give information on the fish's surroundings.*

the pulsed species have their signals in distinctive patterns that are repeated over long periods, sometimes 10–20 minutes. *Gnathonemus petersii*, for example, the elephant-trunk fish of Africa, has a characteristically coded discharge rate which rises slightly after 25 milliseconds, then drops and rises again steeply at 100 milliseconds, and then tails off at 250 milliseconds.

The knifefish, *Sternopygus macrurus* is a wave species and broadcasts at 50–150 Hertz, whereas the nerve-derived *Apternonotus albifrons* uses the 750–1250 Hertz waveband. Within that range males and females choose different frequencies. Male *Sternopygus* signal at 50–90 Hertz, while the females are at 100–150 Hertz. *Sternopygus* also has a different frequency for youngsters who live in nests guarded by the parents and transmit an intermediate 80 Hertz signal. During sexual or aggressive encounters the frequency rises sharply or, on occasion, the signalling stops altogether. There are even 'attack patterns'. And, if two fishes broadcasting at the same frequency meet, they avoid jamming by shifting their signal frequency slightly.

One off-beat application of this work is being studied in Coburg, West Germany, where Bernd Holger Zippe has patented a water-pollution monitoring kit using elephant-trunk fish. It turns out that the fish are sensitive to very small amounts of contaminants, and respond by reducing the frequency of their electric discharge considerably. This can be monitored very simply by placing electrodes in the water and picking up the changes in discharge rate.

The kits, with electrodes and suitable monitoring gear, are available for about £10,000 each. It seems likely that weak-electric fish could soon be the environmental 'watchdogs', or 'watchfish', monitoring water pollution in lakes and rivers all over the globe.

# The Sixth Sense

For centuries people have wanted to believe in a paranormal ability that constitutes the sixth sense, and at one time or another extrasensory perception, telepathy, psychokinesis, or water-divining have been given pseudo-scientific respectability in order to satisfy that need. Even bats were thought, in the sixteenth century, to find their way in the dark by some mystical means that was labelled a 'sixth sense'. But in 1855 Dr Alex von Middendorff proposed what he thought at the time a more tangible candidate for a 'sixth sense' – magnetism.

He was not taken seriously and was heavily criticised for his magnetic hypothesis, but gradually evidence began to accumulate that animals were able to find their way home, over unknown lands and seas, by the most direct route. Somehow they knew in which direction to head. Visual, auditory, or smell maps were denied them, as they had not been through the area before, but one piece of information that *could* tell them where they were and where they should be going, anywhere on the surface of the planet, was their position in relation to the earth's magnetic field.

Papers began to appear in *Nature* describing the homing skills of cats, dogs and even cattle. In 1878 John Vasant wrote to the Academy of Natural Sciences in Philadelphia about a macabre series of observations. He was able to kill small invertebrates with the aid of a magnet. No, not by hitting them with it, but simply by placing the creature in the magnetic field. He described how an unfortunate spider in his living-room succumbed to his interference when positioned between the poles of a horseshoe magnet. The spider stopped, remained motionless, and eventually curled up and died.

But it was in the *Revue Philosphique* in 1882 that Camille Viguier, in a paper entitled '*Le sens d'orientation et ses organes chez les animaux et chez l'homme*', proposed that the earth's magnetic field could be used by migrating birds as a navigational grid.

Almost a hundred years later, a report in the American journal *Science* announced that magnetic material had been found in the abdomens of honey-bees, and a year later similar material was found in the head of the pigeon. As is often the case in science, the ridiculed von Middendorff has been reinstated as a 'man of vision', and his 'sixth sense' proposal that animals might have the ability to detect and appreciate the earth's magnetic field is emerging as a reality.

Central to the story is the mysterious and powerful lodestone – an iron-rich rock, known more formally as magnetite or ferric oxide – which, as part of primitive compass-needles, guided ancient mariners, and particles of which have been found in a variety of living things.

## Bacteria

University of New Hampshire microbiologist, Richard Blakemore, was peering down the microscope at a sample of bacteria taken from the brackish water sediments below Cedar swamp and Eel pond, near Woods Hole, Massachusetts, when he noticed that many of the organisms were swimming in the same direction and had accumulated on one side of the slide.

He turned the instrument round, changed the light source, and moved it to another room, but still the bacteria moved in the same geographical direction. If a magnet was placed next to the slide the bacteria would head towards the pole that would attract the north-pointing end of a compass-needle. Blakemore considered that the bacteria, in their natural habitat, might be influenced by the earth's magnetic field.

Together with Ralf Wolfe, of the University of Illinois, Blakemore was able to isolate and culture one of the bacteria from the sediments, an organism which acquired the name *Aquaspirillum magnetotacticum*. It has a flagellum at each end, and can swim both backwards and forwards, depending on which end you consider the front.

Richard Frankel, of the Francis Bitter National Magnet Laboratory at the Massachusetts Institute of Technology, and Adrianus Kalmijn, then at the Woods Hole Oceanographic Institution, joined Blakemore and Wolfe to examine the spirillum's structure, form and magnetic properties. They found that every bacterium, cultured in an iron-rich medium, contained about twenty minute cubic or octahedral particles of magnetite, with each particle sheathed in its own membrane. These ran down the long axis of the cell, lined-up with north poles and south poles next to each other 'nose-to-tail' fashion, to make one long dipole or bar magnet. The size of the particles, it turned out, was critical. Each was about 500 ångströms (1 ångström = one ten-millionth of a millimetre), a size which allowed the chain of particles to align with the earth's magnetic field. Any larger, and each little magnet would become independent of its neighbour and cancel out the overall direction of the line. Any smaller, and thermal energy (Brownian motion – the irregular movement of minute particles) would similarly disturb and disorient the particles. *A. magnetotacticum* had evolved just the right size and shape magnets for the job.

Why, though, should a bacterium, that is limited in the distance it might travel, develop a mechanism which is profoundly influenced by something as grand as the earth's magnetic field? The answer is that it needs to locate which way is *down. A. magnetotacticum* must live at the correct depth in the mud to get the oxygen-depleted sediments and, in order to seek out the best place, the organism must know in which way to head. But, for the infinitely small bacterium *down* is not an easy direction to find. Large animals, like ourselves, have no trouble in finding *down* – we simply leave it to gravity, but gravity is a weak force and only acts upon large objects. How, though, is the earth's *magnetic field* going to help? A reading on a magnetic compass usually gives horizontal, rather than vertical, information. In order to appreciate the solution, we must consider the shape of the earth's magnetic field.

In 1581 the precision instrument-maker, Robert Norman, built a free-swinging compass-needle that could move in both the vertical and horizontal planes. In London he found that the needle pointed to the north, but with a downward inclination of 70°. Two decades later, in 1600, William Gilbert, physician to Elizabeth I, published *De Magnete Magneticisque Corporibus et de Magno Magnete Tellure* (On the Magnet and Magnetic Bodies and on the Great Magnet the Earth) and revealed the reason for Norman's observation. The magnetosphere, as it is known, is not actually a complete sphere enveloping the earth. At the North and South Poles the magnetic field dips in towards the centre of the planet, like a giant ring doughnut. At the magnetic equator the lines of magnetic force are parallel with the earth's surface, but around the polar 'dimples' the lines gradually tilt downwards. At the pole itself a free-swinging compass would point straight down. The angle of 'dip' is approximately 1° for every 112 kilometres north or south, and this can vary slightly during the day due to varying electrical activity in the upper atmosphere.

Bacteria living at the equator would not benefit from a magnetic sense, as this would receive little vertical information, but those living at more northerly or southerly latitudes can take their bearings from the inclined lines of force and find which way is *down*.

More evidence of magnetic bacteria was sought elsewhere. If the hypothesis is correct there should be south-seeking bacteria in the Southern Hemisphere. New Zealand has about the same angle of magnetic dip as that in New England, and so Blakemore, Kalmijn, Frankel and Nancy Blakemore toured the Antipodes in search of suitable sediments. They found south-seeking bacteria in New Zealand and Tasmania.

Working independently in Australia, Joseph Kirschvink, of Princeton University, found south-seekers in a sewage oxidation pond near Canberra.

Fortaleza, in Brazil, is very near to the magnetic equator, and it came as no surprise to the New Hampshire researchers when their collaborators – F. F. Torres de Araujo, of the University of Ceara, and D. M. S. Esquivel and J. Cannon, of the Brazilian Centre for Physics Research – found both north-seeking and south-seeking bacteria in mud sediments. The organisms moved only horizontally, and it has been suggested that they benefit from their magnetic sense by reducing the tendency to swim upwards. Spirillum bacteria can cover 36 centimetres in a day and would soon enter unsuitable, or even toxic, conditions. It would be of some advantage, also, to move in a preferred direction during foraging, for an individual would be less likely to cross its own path. To the south, at Rio de Janeiro, where the southerly dip is about 25°, only south-seeking bacteria were found.

Experiments, bringing south-seekers to the Northern Hemisphere and vice versa, were carried out. South-seekers in the north headed upwards rather than downwards, and north-seekers in the south followed the same pattern. Research had shown, for the first time, that organisms respond to the earth's magnetic field by means of an internal biomagnetic compass.

## Algae
A Brazilian single-celled green alga, *Chlamydomonas*, is a south-seeker. Like the Woods Hole bacteria, according to Henry G. P. Lins de Barros of the Centro Brasileiro de Pesquisas Fisicas, it orients to the earth's magnetic field probably in order to seek out optimum living conditions in its polluted coastal lagoon near Rio

de Janeiro. Richard Frankel has identified a similar north-seeking alga in Florida waters.

*Chlamydomonas* can gain nutrients in either of two ways – by photosynthesis, for which it would need to be at or near the surface; or by absorbing nutrients from the surrounding waters, in which case it would benefit from being lower down. The magnetotactic algae, it has been suggested, may gain an advantage in being able to use the earth's magnetic field to find their way *down*.

## Coat-of-mail shells

Chitons have magnets on their tongues. That was the intriguing discovery made by Spencer Thorpe, when he examined the teeth on chiton radullae. Chitons are an ancient group of marine molluscs that look a little like segmented worms with eight hard plates along the back. When disturbed they roll up like armadillos. At night chitons forage across the rocks, scraping algae away with their toothed radulla or tongue. At daylight, they return to a precise spot on the rock, where they wait until dark.

Detailed analysis of chiton radulla teeth by Heinz Lowenstam, of the California Institute of Technology, revealed that the tips are made partly of magnetite. Could they be using their magnetic teeth to help them find their own particular spot on the rock?

Jack Tomlinson and his colleagues at San Francisco State University looked at chiton orientation. Californian chitons, it turned out, point predominantly to the north, although orientation was more noticeable in the summer than in the winter. Specimens were put in steel and aluminium containers and seemed to be disoriented when deprived of geomagnetic information in the steel casings. It was also found that the cusps of the radulla teeth would line up with the north end of a bar magnet. If the chitons were floated on small pieces of wood, the entire chiton would align with north.

Similar orientations to the earth's magnetic field were found, in 1822, in the snail *Nassarius obsoletus* and in flatworms.

## Termites

A stroll through the dry outback of northern Australia may bring you to one of nature's remarkable sights – the termitarium of the compass termite. It is like an enormous flat-sided tower block rising as much as 6 metres into the air. Inside live as many as 2 million termites. The human equivalent would be a skyscraper 8 kilometres high.

At the centre of the mound is the royal cell, and entombed within it for her entire life, is the queen – a 13-centimetre long egg factory producing 30,000 eggs day by day for about twenty years. A ring of soldiers guards her and her king. Workers busy about her, bringing food, taking away eggs to the nursery chambers, and cleaning and stroking her rippling, swollen abdomen. The colony is like one gigantic organism, each termite playing its own role to the benefit of the colony as a whole and, in order for the system to function correctly, the microclimate of the mound must be constant. Inside a mound the air might be 15 per cent carbon dioxide, enough to cause a human to lose consciousness. The tall, thin shape of the block would promote the efficient exchange of respiratory gases with the outside world.

Termites do not like it too dry. They prefer working conditions to be hot and humid; but not too hot, 30°C is about right. The entire termitarium is air-conditioned with ventilation shafts and a complicated plumbing system to ensure a constant turnover of the internal atmosphere. Cool air enters at the bottom and warm air leaves from vents in the side or top. Water, as much as 45 litres a day, is sometimes brought from an underground reservoir directly below to evaporate in the chambers and cool the nest. But, with exterior walls as hard and as insulating as concrete on a hot and dry Australian summer's day, the air temperature can be a problem. The compass termite, however, has solved it, partly, in an ingenious way.

Usually, a group of compass termite mounds are found together perhaps tapping a communal underground reservoir, but the remarkable thing is that they all face in exactly the same direction: the narrow faces point to the north and south, and the broad sides face east and west. This means that at midday when the sun at its hottest is directly to the north, the least surface area of mound is exposed. In the cooler early morning and late evening the broad face picks up the maximum amount of solar energy from the sun's rays to warm the colony. Inside the nest, in cooler weather, the termites have been found to aggregate on the side exposed to the sun. If it is too hot they similarly seek the opposite side to the sun, or go deeper down into the subterranean part of the nest.

The mystery is how compass termites know which way to build. Is the answer in the name that we have given them? Can they orient to the points of the compass? Gordon Griggs, of the University of Sydney, examined termite nests in an attempt to find out. If the termites were responding directly to the position of the sun, mounds built in shaded positions were likely to be offset from the general north-south line to compensate for their less favourable position. Griggs, and his colleague A. J. Underwood, looked at fifty nests, some among trees and others in the open, but found very little difference in their orientation. There was very little visible adjustment to local conditions, which led Griggs and Underwood to suggest that termites are genetically programmed to build their nests in the directions observed. There was, though, another puzzle. Accurate measurements revealed that the true long axis of each nest was about 8° away from true north, and not in line with the present magnetic north.

For many years entomologists have suspected that termites are influenced by the earth's magnetic field. The nests of the compass termites in Australia were obvious candidates, and in African termite nests it was known that the queen, in her chamber, stands with her long axis running north-south or directly east-west. Leading termite researcher, Gunther Becker, of the Bundesanstalt für Materialprufung (Berlin-Dahlem) noticed the magnetic response of queen termites of several species quite by accident. A consignment arrived from what was then Rhodesia, and were left overnight. In the morning it was found that they were all aligned in an east-west position. Becker swivelled the box around and returned the following day. The termites had realigned to face east-west once more. Becker carried out a series of experiments and found that termites do, indeed, respond to magnetic fields. If the earth's magnetic field was cancelled, for instance, termite queens would settle down at random. In one laboratory, an alternating magnetic field produced by a heater, which was barely detectable by the scientists' instruments at 20 centimetres, was influencing termites in a plastic container 3 metres away. The termites responded by building their vertical galleries on the side opposite the source.

Another fascinating observation made by Becker involved the individual termites. Each one, it seems, has its own 'biofield' that is used for communication with neighbours. Termite workers placed either side of a 5-millimetre-thick partition of plastic foam could co-ordinate their efforts. When the foam was replaced with aluminium or another metal, communication was interrupted, and co-ordination lost.

## Honey-bees
When a beekeeper sets up his hive he has already determined the orientation of the combs by the position in which he puts the

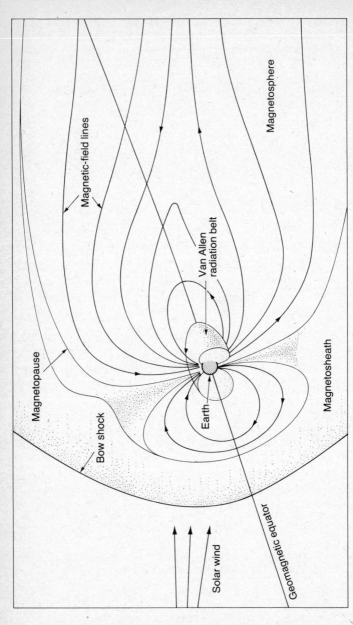

Magnetosphere enveloped by the stream of particles forming the solar wind. Position and orientation of these lines varies according to the time of day and season of year.

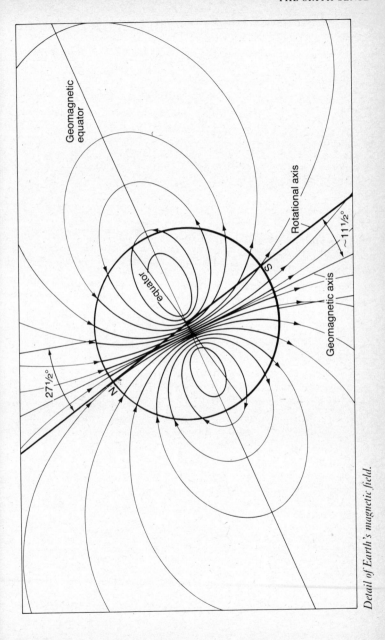

*Detail of Earth's magnetic field.*

wooden comb frames. But what happens in a wild bee nest? How is it that a swarm of bees can decide the direction in which their combs will run? Martin Oehmke of Frankfurt University found the answer when he transferred a swarm from a hive in which the bees built their combs directly north-south, to an artificial hollow tree-trunk in the form of a cardboard cylinder. A flight hole at the centre of the base allowed the bees free access to the outside, otherwise they were in the dark.

Within hours of being introduced to their new home the bees had started to stick lumps of wax all over the box lid and had begun to set up parallel rows of combs. Each comb was aligned in the same north-south direction as those in their original hive. A second experiment in another cylindrical hive confirmed the finding. As all other cues inside the hive had been eliminated, the researchers concluded that the bees had used the only cue that couldn't be removed – the earth's magnetic field.

In a third experiment, Oehmke changed the magnetic field around the cardboard cylinder, deflecting the natural field by 40°. When the bees set up their new home the combs were placed 40° off the original hive setting. In the wild, a magnetic sense would be of considerable value for a swarm of bees entering an old, dark tree-trunk, for they would otherwise have considerable difficulty in co-ordinating the efforts of individuals involved in comb-construction simultaneously at opposite ends of the hollow.

With these tantalising hints, and the success of the magnetic bacteria in mind, honey-bee researchers began to look for signs of a magnetic sense. In 1978 they struck lucky. James Gould, Joseph Kirschvink, and Kenneth Deffeyes, of Princeton University, identified magnetic material in the abdomen of honey-bee workers. It was found to develop in the pupal stage and persist in adults.

Since the initial discovery, bands of cells containing magnetic particles have been found in each abdominal segment, with a concentration just below each segmental ganglion. The detailed work was carried out by Deborah Kuterbach, Benjamin Walcott, and Richard Reeder at the State University of New York at Stony Brook, together with Richard Frankel. They carefully dissected the abdomen and traced the pattern of nerves. From each ganglion a nerve branch was found to enter the bands of magnetic tissue and form a small network of nerve fibres between the cells. Could these minute magnets be twisting to align themselves with the earth's magnetic field and producing a torque that could be picked up by the accompanying nerve cells? The initial crystal settings could have been established when the pupa was motionless in its nursery chamber, when the bee became magnetically 'imprinted'. This would explain Oehmke's results with the cardboard cylinder.

An understanding of the way honey-bees might use a magnetic sense is, as yet, very confused. The key probably lies in the dance of the bees, a remarkable 'language' that is allowing man access to the secrets of honey-bee life.

In 1967 the eminent Austrian zoologist, Karl von Frisch, published a remarkable account of the way that forager bees, returning to the hive, tell others where to go to find the best sources of food. They perform a dance. During the dance, the bee communicates information about the direction of the source with respect to environmental cues – mainly, it is thought, the sun. There are two main dances: a simple circular movement which tells of a food source close to the hive, and the 'waggle' dance for distant sources.

The returning bee enters the hive and starts to move in a curious circular pattern, all the while waggling its abdomen. Such 'extrovert' behaviour attracts the attention of others, and gradually an audience gathers close to the performer, the bees touching her gently with their antennae. The soloist waggles across the comb, at a particular angle, stops waggling, and then circles back to the right, waggles across again, stops waggling, and circles back to the left, and so on. The angle that the waggle section of the dance makes to the vertical represents the angle between the sun's azimuth and the food source. The length of the waggle part and the number of waggles represent the distance, and the intensity of the dance represents the richness of the food supply. In addition, the bee must convert horizontal information into a vertical gravity-influenced pattern because the comb on which it dances is upright.

A food source directly below the position of the sun will elicit an upward-moving vertical waggle. Food located, say, 45° to the east of the sun, will result in a dance that is 45° left of the vertical, and a source 180° away will be communicated in a vertical waggle down the comb.

Curiously, the bearings are not accurately matched. Martin Lindauer and Herman Martin found that a slight misdirection, following a regular diurnal pattern, can occur in the dance. The angle of the gravity-assisted 'waggle run' appears to be influenced and offset by the lines of the earth's magnetic field. The dance can be corrected by cancelling out the field, the bees dancing with respect to gravity only. If the comb is placed horizontally, and the influence of gravity eliminated, the bees are at first confused. When left in this position for about three weeks, subsequent dances pointed preferentially north-south or east-west. Compensation for the geomagnetic field resulted again in complete disorientation.

Jack Tomlinson, Sandra McGinty, and Janis Kish, of San Francisco State University, exposed dancing bees to a localised magnetic source. They found that if a small permanent magnet is placed in the vicinity of a dancing bee, the insect stops dancing.

There are also other questions. What happens if the sun goes in? This is where von Frisch again showed his genius, for he proposed that the honey-bee has a hierarchy of mechanisms for orientation. In short, the bee has a back-up system for when the going gets tough.

On a partly cloudy day, with patches of blue sky, the bee will not see the sun constantly. Also, in the wild, the honey-bee is a forest-dweller and will lose the sun behind the leaf canopy or between the many upright boughs in the wood. Under these conditions, it was found that bees are able to analyse the polarisation of ultraviolet light from the clear sky that could be seen, and work out a bearing on the position of the sun for the purpose of the dance. It is possible that the bees have a 'photographic' record of the general polarised light pattern in the sky, and when communicating the position of the food source, simply match their observed portion of the picture with the overall 'photograph'.

When the sun is completely absent from the sky, on overcast days or in fog, bees still forage and dance. Although visibility, for humans, may be down to a few metres, the honey-bee must continue to collect food if the colony is to survive the winter. Back-up system number two is used.

James Gould and Fred Dyer, at Princeton, believe that on overcast days the bees are able to predict the position of the sun with reference to local landmarks. In one experiment, Gould and Dyer trained bees on a sunny day to find a feeding-station at the end of a row of trees to the north-east of the hive. During the night they moved the hive to a site where a similar row of trees ran about 130° in the opposite direction. The next day the bees ignored the north-easterly sun compass heading and followed the line of trees to the new station. In their dance, though, they communicated the directions to the original feeding-station.

This showed that bees, on cloudy days, memorise the sun's position in the sky by reference to local landmarks. At midday the sun came out and the workers realised the mistake in the dance. They changed the dance angle by about 130° and for the rest of the day used the sun correctly. This also demonstrated the hierarchical nature of bee orientation mechanisms, for the sun when available is the preferred reference point.

There is, however, a slight catch. Wild bees in the visually complex forest, with its superabundance of identical vertical landmarks, may not find a sufficient number of discernible cues to calculate the sun's course. Indeed, in some of von Frisch's experiments in 1950, he noticed that bees transferred to sites with few landmarks would still find feeding-stations at the old compass heading. Could it be that another back-up system is operating, one that relies on the earth's magnetic field?

A vespid wasp, the common housefly, the American cockroach, and the staghorn beetle also join the honey-bee and the termite as 'magnetic' insects.

## Sharks

Several species of shark have been found to migrate great distances across the oceans, but how do they find their way in the vast, apparently featureless sea? Again, an ability to detect and appreciate the earth's magnetic field seems to be the answer.

In 1917 G. H. Parker and A. P. Van Heusen, at Harvard University, recorded that a catfish, known as the common brown bullhead, responded to metallic rods placed several centimetres from its head, but paid no attention to glass ones. They showed that the behaviour was related to the generation of galvanic currents at the interface between metal and water, but took the work no further.

Then in 1934, Sven Dijkgraaf, of the University of Utrecht, found that small blindfolded sharks would turn away from a piece of rusty steel wire placed in the water near their heads. They would ignore a similar test with a glass rod. Dijkgraaf reasoned that electrical currents generated by the metal were being detected by the sharks. Adrianus Kalmijn, a student of Dijkgraaf, discovered the sharks' sensitivity to be quite incredible. In his experiments, they were able to detect electrical fields as weak as a flashlight battery connected to terminals 1,600 kilometres apart. Dijkgraaf and Kalmijn in Utrecht, and Richard Murray at the University of Birmingham, showed that the part of the shark that responds to electrical fields are the ampullae of

Lorenzini, tiny jelly-filled pits that cover the snout of sharks. In 1971 Kalmijn discovered that one function of this ability to detect weak electrical fields is the capture of prey. All living marine organisms are surrounded by electrical fields. This results from different electrical potentials on various parts of the skin which produce electrical currents in water. Sharks, it was found, can detect these fields and use them to home-in on their prey. In laboratory experiments, flatfish buried in the sand were found relatively easily by a small shark.

Experiments in the open sea with an underwater test-rig demonstrated that sharks preferred to bite at live electrodes set either side of an odour source, rather than at the source itself. The small sharks would use their keen olfactory sense to follow the odour trail into the rig, but would veer off at about 25 centimetres to attack the live electrode. If it was switched off and the electrode on the other side switched on, the shark would circle for a while and then bite at the second electrode.

It has also been noticed that when large sharks, like great white sharks, go in for their final bite, a membrane covers the eye to protect it from struggling prey. The shark swims blind, guided to the target only by sensing the electrical field. Skin-divers in shark cages have been scared by great whites attacking the bars of flotation tanks. John McCosker, of San Francisco's Steinhart Aquarium, believes the sharks have been confused by the electrical fields generated by the metals in the cage. Often they will swim off, apparently in a complete frenzy, and attack other metallic objects like propellers.

But remarkable as these findings are, they are only part of the story of the shark's electrical sense. The ampullae of Lorenzini are concerned also with orientation and navigation.

The first tests carried out by Kalmijn at the Scripps Institution of Oceanography were with leopard sharks in a circular fibreglass tank. A small induction coil was placed to one side of the tank in such a way that it would interfere with the sharks' normal circular swimming pattern around the periphery. The current was switched on when the sharks were at the far side of the pool but, in reaching the coil, they would veer off to the centre of the pool.

A chance observation led to the second experiment. It was noticed that early in the morning all the sharks were gathered at one side of the pool. The pool was covered with black plastic sheeting, to eliminate visual cues, but the sharks were still found in a group at one side. The researchers then tricked the sharks.

With two large induction coils around the tank the earth's magnetic field was ostensibly neutralised. Next morning the sharks were distributed randomly about the tank. Clearly, sharks could sense the earth's magnetic field, but having detected it, how would they use it?

Ocean currents induce electrical currents as they pass through the earth's magnetic field. The electrical current is perpendicular to the line of magnetic force and of sufficient strength to be detected by a shark. In tests with a close relative of the shark family, another elasmobrach fish – the sting-ray – it was found that the direction in which the ray would swim in a tank and seek a reward was dependent on the polarity of electric current passed through the body of sea water.

In addition, as the shark swims through the water and through the earth's magnetic field, it generates local electric fields. The way that the current drops in strength as it gets further and further away from the fish (the voltage gradient) depends on the direction in which the fish is moving. The voltage gradient is related to compass heading, giving the shark its own electromagnetic compass sense.

This has led Adrianus Kalmijn, and, independently, workers at the Pavlov Institute of Physiology in Leningrad, to surmise that sharks, the related skates and rays, and the 'primitive' ratfish (which also possess the ampullae) are able to find their way in the sea using an electromagnetic sense.

## Tuna

Another marine creature known to travel over vast distances is the tuna. Propelled through the water by muscles that are kept warmer than the temperature of the surrounding sea water, these fast, sleek fish can migrate about 300 kilometres in a day. In bursts they can reach speeds of 64 kilometres an hour. A magnetic sense for trans-oceanic migration has been hinted at for some time, but it wasn't until 1980 that Andrew Dixon, Michael Walker and Joseph Kirschvink took yellow-fin tunas into a research tank at the National Marine Fisheries Service in Hawaii, and a magnetic sense was confirmed.

The researchers were able to train four tunas to swim through a plastic frame by rewarding them with food. Two of the fish were trained to swim through the frame when the magnetic field around the tank was normal, and two were trained to pass through only when the field was increased substantially. The tunas performed well and would only swim through the frame when experiencing the appropriate strength magnetic field. Whether the fish were responding to intensity or direction of the magnetic field was not clear.

Further confirmation that a magnetic sense is involved came from dissection of a tuna head. Magnetite was found in association with nerve fibres in tissue above the ethmoid bone (in humans the bone on which the nose sits). Magnetic particles have been found in yellow-fin, skipjack and kawakawa tuna, and in blue marlins.

Although magnetic material has not been found in the salmon, Ronald Merrill, Ernest Brannon and Thomas Quin, of the University of Washington, have shown that sockeye salmon navigate through lakes by using the earth's magnetic field.

## Salamanders

Salamanders can find their way home even in the dark, according to Cornell University biologist, Kraig Adler, and they do it with the aid of the earth's magnetic field. Salamanders were captured and taken in light-tight boxes away from their pond. No matter which of their senses was covered or blocked out, the salamanders would unerringly head in the direction of home.

Weak electrical fields around their boxes would confuse at first but eventually the animals would compensate and head off once more in the right direction. Kraig and his colleagues found that the magnetic homing sense of the salamander is many times more sensitive than that of the pigeon.

## Birds

Racing pigeons have been known to take just one day to find their way back to the home loft from a release point some 1,000 kilometres away. They have travelled at about 80 kilometres per hour on average. In order to achieve such a speedy return, the birds would have little time for random searching, and would have followed a direct flight-path, a process requiring both a compass and a map.

This extraordinary navigation skill is all the more intriguing when it is realised that the racing pigeon is a domesticated version of the rock dove *Columba livia*, a species of bird that shows very little seasonal migration, except around the Sahara. Racing pigeons, though, were bred rigorously in Belgium in the nineteenth century. Much money changes hands in pigeon-breeding circles on the basis of which bird finishes first. Speedy birds are bred, slow ones end up in the oven!

The homing pigeon has been in use for over 2,000 years. They were first bred as message carriers, when the armies of the Persians, Assyrians, Egyptians, Phoenicians and Romans used them for communication from the battlefield. In this century pigeons were used in both world wars.

Part of the birds' training was to take them progressively greater distances from the loft in order to familiarise them with the local topography. As recently as thirty years ago it was thought that familiarisation was the answer to bird navigation, although there had been tantalising hints since the late nineteenth century, from people like Viguier, that there was more to it than met the eye.

Donald Griffin (of bat fame) chased after gannets in light aircraft in order to follow migrants in the air. It became clear that birds could not migrate by landmarks alone. At sea, islands are too few and changes in sea colour, salinity, and temperature are too variable. On moonless nights, landmarks disappear altogether. Familiarisation, as the complete answer, was finally knocked on the head when it was revealed that adult cuckoos fly off to Africa a couple of months before their offspring. The young birds could not possibly memorise a route, with its landmarks, when they have not been on the journey before. An inbuilt navigation system must be involved.

There was also mounting evidence that migrating birds unerringly found their way back to the exact breeding-site that they had left the previous year. Swallows, for example, locate last year's nest and re-use it. In one classic experiment, Geoffrey Matthews, director of research at the Wildfowl Trust, demonstrated the incredible navigational talents of two Manx shearwaters. They were taken from their burrows on the Welsh island of Skokholm and transported to Boston and Venice where they were released. Travelling at 392 and 426 kilometres a day respectively, often over unfamiliar terrain or featureless ocean, the two birds returned to the very same nesting burrows from which they had been taken. How on earth could they do it? A celestial compass was, perhaps, the obvious explanation. The sun, the moon and the stars have been used for centuries by human travellers, why not then by birds?

In the 1950s Gustav Kramer and Franz Sauer, of the Max Planck Institute, showed that birds could orient to the sun and the stars. Kramer first noticed that starlings in a cage take an interest in the northerly part of the cage in spring, the direction, in the wild, of their springtime north-westerly migration. A screen placed around the cage, but still allowing a view of the sky, did not stop the behaviour, and so it was concluded that landmarks are not involved.

A circular cage with mirrors was constructed and the starlings were exposed both to the direct rays of the sun, and to the sun reflected in mirrors. Whether observing the direct sun or a reflected sun in a different direction, the starlings maintained the same angle to the sun. This angle varied with the time of day, which showed that the birds compensated for the sun traversing the sky, and also appreciated the passage of time by some internal clock.

The biological clock of pigeons was put to good use in experiments conducted by Klaus Schmidt-Koenig, of the University of Göttingen, when he shifted their diurnal rhythms. The midday sun is considered to be south by birds in the Northern Hemisphere. Released birds will head for home in the usual direct way. If, however, the bird's clock is advanced by six hours, the expected noon setting is treated as west, rather than south. These birds tend to fly 90° to the left of their home. When the sun was *not* visible, however, phase-shifted birds headed straight for home.

These experiments indicated several things. First, the phase-shifting experiments in sunlight showed that a bird's navigational system is in two parts – an orientation map, which told the bird where it was in relation to its destination, and a sun compass which told it how to get there. Secondly the bird could not see the sun through the clouds nor appreciate polarised light cues from patches of blue sky, or it would have headed in the wrong direction. Thirdly, the tests demonstrated that the basic orientation map must be something unaffected by changes in the bird's internal biological clock – such as the sun, moon and stars.

Franz Sauer carried out orientation experiments under the night sky. Using warblers in a planetarium he was able to show that birds adjusted their direction if he rotated the artificial night sky. Even birds that had been hatched in an incubator and had never seen the real sky would orient to the star pattern above. At Cornell University Stephen Emlen, in the summer of 1972, placed indigo buntings *Passerina cyanea* in a planetarium and projected a night sky that revolved around a star in the constellation of Orion, rather than the usual pole-star. In the autumn, the birds were exposed to the novel sky rotation and showed directional tendencies appropriate to that sky. This showed that young birds need not inherit a star *map*, but could learn a star *compass*, and were perfectly well able to navigate with a novel night sky.

The importance of learning in navigation was demonstrated with migrating starlings by the Dutch researcher, Albert Perdeck, of the Ecological Research Station at Arnhem. Ringing experiments had shown that eastern Baltic starlings travelled to the Netherlands on their way to the British Isles or France. Perdeck intercepted a thousand or so and took them to Switzerland for release. This simulated what might happen during a storm with the group being blown off course. Adult and immature birds were released separately. The young birds resumed a course parallel to their original flight-path, heading for Spain and southern France. The more experienced birds headed for their normal wintering grounds in northern Europe. Although the birds had inherited a tendency to fly in a particular direction, it was clear that there was a learned component necessary for accurately locating their destination. Normally, mixed flocks of adults and juveniles fly together, one group perhaps learning from the other.

What, though, was the nature of the inherited component? Indeed, how do birds fare when the sun, moon and stars are obscured by clouds or fog? Many birds just put down and wait for better weather, but not all. Pigeons have shown that when the sky is overcast they can still find their way home. Could they be using a magnetic sense?

Italian researchers say not. At the University of Pisa, Floriano Papi and his colleagues propose an olfactory system. Scents from air currents learned at the loft guide pigeons back to their home, they suggest. American researchers have consistently failed to reproduce these experiments, although an olfactory element in navigation, possibly close to the loft, cannot be ruled out.

For many years bird navigation has been dominated by a sun-arc hypothesis as the basic grid-map from which birds navigate. A bird, so the argument goes, can work out its position on the earth's surface relative to its destination by recognising the sun's arc, and measuring how far along the arc the sun has travelled. It then compares this information with a prediction of the same calculations at the destination – and all this in a couple of minutes. Evidence to support the theory has been slim.

In fact, evidence seems to be taking biologists back to Viguier's hypothesis. Although sun and star compasses appear to have a role in direction-finding, the basic map or navigational grid is, perhaps, turning out to be related to the earth's magnetic field. It is certainly involved in determining a compass heading.

In 1971 William Keeton, of Cornell University, fastened magnets on to the backs of pigeons and demonstrated that they were unable to orient on overcast days. Similar-sized brass bars had no effect.

Charles Walcott and Robert Green, of the State University of New York at Stony Brook, placed small coils either side of a pigeon's head. Powered by a minute mercury battery, the coils could be used to produce a controllable earth strength magnetic field. By reversing the polarity of the field, a pigeon could be made to fly in the opposite direction to its home. Three years later, Keeton and his colleagues found that minute fluctuations in the earth's magnetic field, as small as a five-hundredth of the natural field, would upset a bird's compass heading.

This was significant, for previous studies had indicated a link between sunspot activity and the speed with which racing pigeons returned to their home base; and sun spots are known to affect the magnetosphere, causing measurable fluctuations in the earth's magnetic field. Slow-returning birds, i.e. those having orientation difficulties, were more noticeable on days following sunspot activity.

Many observers have recorded the same disorientation problems in migrating birds that have encountered magnetic storms or anomalies. Pigeons released in the iron-ore rich Kyffhauser Mountains in East Germany, set off in the opposite direction to their lofts before rectifying their mistake.

Migrating birds flying over a large alternating-current radar antennae system in Wisconsin were found, by Ronald Larkin and Pamela Sutherland, of Rockefeller University, to change altitude or turn suddenly when the equipment was operating. Strangely, magnetic disturbances cause birds to deflect to the left. Furthermore, many of the magnetic disturbance disorientations were on sunny days, when the birds were presumably using their sun compass.

There are other curious inconsistencies in the story. The pigeons fitted with earth-strength magnetic coils or bar magnets did not respond to the disorienting magnetic field on sunny days, but flew normally, although the strength of the coil or magnet was many magnitudes greater than any anomaly the bird might pass. They were, nonetheless, disoriented when in the vicinity of a magnetic anomaly. Might this mean that the bird's orientation grid is based on fluctuations in the magnetic field rather than its strength?

On sunny days, however, *young* birds *are* disrupted by magnets, indicating that the sun compass is probably learned. In clock-shift tests young birds have been shown not to use the sun compass, but they can orient nevertheless. Roswitha and Wolfgang Wiltschko and Donatus Nohr, at Frankfurt University, denied a test group of homing pigeons the sun before midday. When they were released, the birds could not use the sun compass in the mornings. When fitted with magnets they became disoriented, indicating a magnetic compass in use.

At the University of Lund, Thomas Alerstam and Göran Högstedt altered the geomagnetic field around the nests of pied flycatchers, *Ficedula hypoleuca*, during the incubation and nestling periods. Two months later they saw a complementary shift in migratory orientation at the start of the southward journey – more evidence to support the hypothesis that the magnetic sense may provide a primary, innate reference frame. In view of the fact that birds learn a sun compass later in life, is it logical to consider magnetic orientation as a means of calibrating other celestial cues?

In Frankfurt, Wiltschko and Freidrich Merkel found that robins, *Erithacus rubecula*, like Blakemore's bacteria, may use the inclination of the earth's magnetic field for orientation by sensing the angle between the magnetic lines of force and the direction of gravity. The smallest angle between the two is north. Also at Frankfurt, Wolfgang Veihmann found that the blackcap *Sylvia atricapilla* uses a magnetic sense. Birds within a closed aviary would flutter towards the south in autumn, but if the magnetic field around the cage was turned, the birds changed direction. William Southern, of Northern Illinois University, reported that ring-billed gulls are influenced by magnetic activity.

Another curiosity, though, was that birds transported to the release site in disturbed magnetic conditions, like the back of a car or inside a coil, were less able to orient. Could it be that test birds actually memorise every twist and turn as they travel through the earth's magnetic field?

But, where is the magnetic receptor? How does a bird get its geomagnetic information? The early bar-magnet experiments gave a clue – the part involved seemed to be in the head or neck. In 1979 Charles Walcott, at Stony Brook, and James Gould and Joseph Kirschvink at Princeton, discovered magnetite in the heads of pigeons.

In each pigeon dissected, the research team found magnetite

in tissue between the dura mater and the skull. The tissue itself contained nerve fibres. At the California Institute of Technology a year later, David Presti and John Pettigrew similarly located magnetic material in the neck muscles of pigeons and migratory white-crowned sparrows, *Zonotrichia leucophrys*. They proposed that a geomagnetic receptor might involve the coupling of the magnetic material to muscle spindles, sensory structures that are sensitive to stretch, and which play an important role in the regulation of muscle movement. This was an interesting observation for, previously, researchers with pigeons in the laboratory could not reproduce any physiological changes, such as changes in heart-rate, in response to magnetic interference. Only flying birds played the game. Michael Bookman, of the Massachussets Institute of Technology though, had noticed that he *could* get a response from laboratory birds if they were encouraged to flutter on short flights and move their heads during the tests. Electro-physiological experiments are now needed to ascertain the location and mechanism of the bird's magnetic sense but, if and when the magnetic receptor is identified, the fundamental questions still remain – does the bird have a magnetic map? It is clear that the earth's magnetic field could provide positional and directional information. Inclination of the field or 'dip' and field strength could be used to construct a bi-co-ordinate map. But there is one final and intriguing problem. Many migrating birds fly from the Northern to the Southern Hemisphere and back again during their biannual wanderings. What happens to their magnetic sense when they cross the magnetic equator?

## Whales and dolphins

Orkney, Shetland and The Wash are 'accident black-spots' for whales. Of 137 live whale strandings around the British Isles in the past seventy years analysed by Margaret Klinowska, of Cambridge University, many have occurred in these areas. Geologically these stranding sites are interesting for they are places where lines of geometric variations, known as 'magnetic valleys', cross the coastline or are blocked by islands. Could it be that whales are using geomagnetic cues, much like an automatic pilot, to guide them through the sea? The suggestion is that whales are swimming along with their other sensory systems, like echo location and vision, switched off. When they reach a 'magnetic valley' which coincides with a sand bank or a beach, the whales are caught unawares, and suddenly find a sandy shore beneath them which they didn't expect to be there. Disoriented and confused in their topographical trap, they continually swim into the shore.

There is some circumstantial evidence to support the theory. When the number of coastal species involved in live strandings is compared with the number of deep-water species, most inshore dolphins have already died, probably due to 'natural' causes, before their bodies are washed up on the beach. Only 6 per cent, for example, of harbour porpoises have stranded live in the past few decades. False killer whales, an offshore species less able to negotiate unfamiliar inshore waters, represent 67 per cent of British strandings.

A magnetic sense for dolphins was realised as a possibility in 1981, when J. Zoeger of Los Angeles Harbor College, and J. R. Dunn and M. Fuller, of the University of California at Santa Barbara, discovered particles of a magnetic material in the brain of Pacific dolphins, *Delphinus delphis*. Dead dolphins that had washed up on Californian beaches were obtained from the Los Angeles County Museum of Natural History and were dissected. Sections were cut across the head and placed in a magnetometer. Magnetic tissue, containing particles of magnetite mostly, was found in a membrane near the junction of the cerebrum with the cerebellum. In one specimen the disc-like magnetite particle could be seen to be associated with a net of fibres, probably nerve fibres, and a stalk-like projection, possibly a magnetic receptor.

The association of the fibres and the particles suggested to the researchers that the magnetite was not merely a bi-product of metabolism but must have a function in dolphin life. They speculated that the tissue was, indeed, a magnetic field receptor and could be aiding the dolphin in orientation and navigation. The material, though, was magnetically 'soft', and could not be considered as analogous to a compass-needle, although its fragile nature might indicate that it could be affected by the earth's magnetic field.

Similarly sited magnetic tissues have also been found in the head of a Cuvier's beaked whale.

## Humans

We have magnetite in our ethmoid cavities. So say Robin Baker and Jan Mather, of Manchester University, who found magnetic particles near the noses of humans and rodents. Kirschvink reported magnetite in the same place in monkeys. In all cases the particles were associated with nerve fibres. Does this mean that man, too, has a magnetic sense? Robin Baker thinks we have. He took blindfolded students miles away into the wild and asked them to point out the direction of their home. Surprisingly, students pointed more accurately with the blindfold still on than when they took it off.

Baker repeated the experiments with a group of sixteen and seventeen-year-old schoolchildren. Some wore helmets with bar magnets attached and others wore helmets with brass bars as substitutes. Those wearing the magnets were noticeably disoriented.

In a third series of tests the bar-magnet helmets were replaced with specially designed PVC helmets with Helmholtz coils. Some were rigged to give a left-shifted magnetic field, others were shifted to the right, still others were switched off. Again, the control group with unactivated helmets was significantly better at pointing to home. Female subjects did better than males.

Could this mean we really have a sixth sense? Unfortunately, other researchers are having difficulty in repeating the experiments so we shall have to wait and see. There is, however, one more interesting point to be made. The discovery by Presti and Pettigrew of magnetite particles in association with muscles in the necks of pigeons, may have some significance in waterdivining or dowsing. The slight flickering of a stick could be related to changes in the local magnetic field. Dowsers hold their divining instruments in such a way that any minute muscle movement will cause a flick of the wrists. A magnetically sensitive receptor might give rise to the traditional dowsing response.

# Living Lights

Carrier-based aircrews in the South Pacific, returning at night from their Second World War bombing missions, were able to find their ships in the darkness simply by locating and following the lines of 'phosphorescence' in the wake. Sir Walter Scott noticed it too. In his 'Lord of the Isles' he wrote:

*Awak'd before the rushing prow,*
*The mimic fires of ocean glow,*
*Those lightnings of the wave;*
*Wild sparkles crest the broken tides,*
*And flashing round, the vessel's sides*
*With elfish lustre lave;*
*While far behind, their livid light*
*To the dark billows of the night*
*A blooming splendour gave.*

C. W. Thomson recalls in his *Voyage on the Challenger*, the sea south-east of the Cape Verde Islands:

There was no moon, and although the night was perfectly clear and the stars shone brightly, the lustre of the heavens was fairly eclipsed by that of the sea. The unbroken part of the surface appeared pitch black, but wherever there was the least ripple the whole line broke into a brilliant crest of clear white light.

What caused these incredible displays remained a mystery for many centuries, although writers like Anaximenes (500 BC), and Pliny (AD 50) had described luminescence in marine creatures such as the common piddock *Pholas*, a mollusc that bores into limestone rocks. In the seventeenth century Descartes proposed that as a wave passes across the surface of the water, sparks are generated by the separation of particles of salt from particles of water. Robert Boyle, similarly, proffered a friction hypothesis, this time between the waves and the atmosphere.

Putrefaction had its supporters. These ideas emerged at the

same time as Boyle's work on inorganic chemiluminescence associated with rotting wood and meat. Theories involving chemical reactions with phosphorous were popular, and indeed, the phenomenon of sea-glow became known as 'phosphorescence'. In the eighteenth century, eminent chemist George Wilson was persuaded to look at the luminescence of the sea-pen *Pennatula*. He wrote:

> On the whole, I believe it most probable that the animal secretes a spontaneously inflammable substance. It may be a compound of phosphorous, but it is not necessary to assume that it is.

Benjamin Franklin thought that 'phosphorescence' in the sea might be an electrical discharge caused by the interaction of the salt and water, although in 1750 he was puzzled when he noticed that it ceased if the water had been kept for a long time. In the same year two Italian naturalists, Vianelli and Grixellini, from Venice, discovered that the sparkle in disturbed water was due to the single-celled dinoflagellate *Noctiluca*.

Dinoflagellates are the red algae responsible for 'red tides'. These are blooms of algae that, at certain times of the year, account for the deaths of large numbers of fish in the sea and of customers in shellfish restaurants. They are ubiquitous in the oceans and glow when mechanically or electrically disturbed. Each algal flash of light lasts for about one-tenth of a second. Why though, should they flash at all?

Luminescence occurs only at night. The emission of light is insufficient during the day to be noticeable. There is a definite circadian cycle which peaks at night and can be reproduced in the laboratory in conditions of continual darkness. In some locations, notably Oyster Bay, Jamaica and Baia Fosforescente, Puerto Rico, the light is so bright it competes favourably with moonlight, and attracts the attention of the island's tourists.

Zooplankton like to feed at night. Copepod crustaceans, particularly, graze on the rich dinoflagellate soup. Light, though, appears to startle these little creatures and so the dinoflagellates flash in order to escape. Research has shown that copepods encountering flashing dinoflagellates swim more erratically than those about to gobble up non-luminous prey. There is also the suggestion that large numbers of phosphorescent dinoflagellates, activated by small prey animals, draw attention to themselves. The light produced attracts larger predators that mop up and eliminate the algal grazers. This 'burglar-alarm' flashing system is therefore an effective means of escape.

More recently, Charles Galt, of the California State University of Long Beach, suggested that other creatures also contribute to 'phosphorescence'. He noticed that flashes of light are produced by larvaceans (Urochordates) when mechanically stimulated. These creatures are abundant, like the dinoflagellates, in the plankton at the surface of the oceans. Indeed, they are thought to rival the copepods in actual numbers in the zooplankton of coastal waters. Studies with the larvacean *Oikopleura dioica* revealed that not only was the animal itself luminescent but also its discarded mucous 'houses'.

Interestingly, larvaceans and dinoflagellates have caught the quizzical eye of defence strategists employed by the world's navies. Warships moving across the surface of the sea at night are clearly visible from the air. Submarines, it seems, leave a tell-tale trail of 'phosphorescence' as they travel below the waves, and there is a reseach programme with military satellites aimed at using the phenomenon to pinpoint them in the oceans. A communications system between submarines making use of lasers has hit a snag, though. Blue-green light is the best colour for transmission through sea water and that's the part of the spectrum already jammed by the signals of marine creatures.

Until the eighteenth century most of the organisms known to produce their own light were terrestrial ones, such as fireflies and glow-worms. Subsequent observations have revealed an enormous diversity of animal and plant groups that show bioluminescence – bacteria, fungi, red algae, jellyfish, worms, snails, squid, shrimps, fireflies, sharks and bony fish – and most live in the sea, a fact that might give some clues about the origin and evolution of bioluminescence, a process that seems to have evolved unaccountably many times in living things.

## Cold light

The incandescent electric light bulb that we have in the home produces light and a considerable amount of heat. It is only 10 per cent efficient. Bioluminescent organisms produce their light without heat and are nearly 100 per cent efficient. It is a chemical process in which the substance luciferin is oxidised, in the presence of the enzyme luciferase, to oxyluciferin. The energy released during that reaction is held by the oxyluciferin molecule for a split second, when it is deemed to be in an excited state. The energy is finally liberated as light in the visible part of the spectrum. No heat is produced. It is a cold light.

In 1887 Raphael Dubois coined the term luciferin – from Lucifer, the light-bearer – and proposed that luciferase is the enzyme involved in chemiluminescent reactions. But detailed chemical analyses were not undertaken until much later when E. Newton Harvey of Princeton University found that the chemical reactions are not identical in all bioluminescent organisms, although they all follow the same luciferin-luciferase pattern. If the chemical components of two unrelated species are mixed together, no light is produced. There seem to be very subtle chemical differences in the structure of the molecules involved. One manifestation of the chemical diversity is the colour of the light. Shrimps, for instance, have a deep-blue light, dinoflagel-lates tend towards the yellows, and one firefly species has a red light.

The substances also have very complicated chemical struc-tures. William McElroy and Howard Seliger, of Johns Hopkins University, worked out the structure of firefly luciferin and luciferase. The latter turned out to have over 1,000 sub-units, becoming one of the largest and most complicated proteins to have been analysed. The same workers proposed an origin for bioluminescence.

In the first three-quarters of the earth's life history, the dominant life forms were anaerobic bacteria. Then along came the blue-green algae that upset the environment by producing, as a product of photosynthesis, vast quantities of oxygen which would have been toxic to the bacteria. In order to offset this toxicity the anaerobic bacteria might have made some metabolic changes, in particular, to remove oxygen. Chemiluminescence in some bacteria today may be a relic from primordial times.

## Bacterial partners

It has been estimated that about 90 per cent of the animals living in the mid-water portion of the sea are able to produce light, but there is a growing awareness that it is not the animal itself that is making the light, but symbiotic bacteria.

There are two groups of bacteria that are known to be light emitters – *Beneckea*, free-living forms, and *Photobacterium*, symbionts with squid, fish and a multitude of other marine creatures. These minute organisms glow over the entire cell and continuously, but only when there is a sufficient number packed into an area, and only when the critical amount of luminescence-inducing substance is produced.

Until recently it was thought that some of the luminous fish and cephalopods produced their own light without the help of bacteria, but in 1980, Gary Leisman, Daniel Cohn and Kenneth Nealson, of the Scripps Institution of Oceanography, reported that even these systems owe their glow to luminescent bacteria. The clue was the speed with which bacterial luciferase activity decays during the light-producing reaction. *Photobacterium*, unlike its free-living cousin, has what is known as 'fast-decay kinetics', and it is this factor that can be used to identify a bacterial origin for the luminescence. The Scripps research team took extracts of the light-producing organs of several squid and fishes that were previously thought to produce their own light and found that they exhibited fast-decay kinetics. In some species the light organs contain bacteria-like structures, known as bacteroids, but it has not been possible to culture bacteria from the extracts. Could this represent an evolutionary stage in the symbiotic association that is one step further than having the bacteria actually present? The research team has speculated that by studying the continuum of bacterial symbioses in light organs, an understanding of the evolution of symbiosis itself might be achieved.

## Jewels of the deep

The German marine biologist, Carl Chun, was on a cruise in the Indian Ocean in 1903 when two small diadem squids were hauled to the surface from a great depth. He called them 'jewelled wonder-torches' and wrote:

> One would think that the body was adorned with a diadem of brilliant gems. The middle organs of the eyes shone with ultramarine blue, the lateral ones with a pearly sheen. Those towards the front of the lower surface of the body gave out a ruby red light, while those behind were snowy-white or pearly, except the median one, which was sky-blue.

Squid and other cephalopods (the group of animals that includes octopus, squid, cuttlefish and pearly nautilus) exhibit their luminescence in any of three ways – from bacteria-filled glands, from photophores, or in luminous clouds. The sepioid cuttlefish *Sepiola* has light organs equipped with both lens and reflector. The squid *Abralia* has photophores over the entire body, while the deep-sea squid *Bathothauma* has light organs on the eye which are on the end of stalks. *Histioteuthis* and *Calliteuthis* have an enormous left eye with few associated light organs, and a small right eye encircled by them. Why this should be, nobody knows, although it has been speculated that there is some link between the assymetry and the vertical movement of the creatures to and from the dark, deep sea and brighter waters.

A function for light organs in squid must, of necessity, be speculative. Direct behavioural observations are, at present, almost impossible in the deep sea. *Chiroteuthis*, with light organs on the tips of the tentacles alone, is likely to be using its light as a lure. The animal is a poor swimmer and is unlikely to be dashing around the ocean chasing its prey. Gilbert Voss, in Miami, suggested that the squid dangles its tentacles below its body, planktonic organisms are attracted by the light and are then caught on the pad of hooked suckers and hauled up to the mouth.

Each species of squid has a different pattern of light organs, and so light displays might have an important function in courtship. The lights may help in the initial location of individuals, and then, in attraction. One species, the firefly squid *Watasenia scintillans*, discovered in Japanese waters by the zoologist Shozaburo Watasé, flashes its light periodically. The entire body of the 10-centimetre-long squid is covered in photophores which flash a very bright bluish light – 'like the stars in heaven' reflects Watasé, and under the microscope each photophore flash 'is so brilliant that it seems like a sunbeam shot through a tiny hole in a window curtain'. Like its namesake, the firefly, could these displays function as courtship signals? It seems likely.

A 'squirt-and-dash' strategy, for defence, is the obvious explanation for the way that some species of cephalopods discharge a luminous cloud of mucus into the water. The first to be discovered was *Heteroteuthis dispar*, a sepioid about the size of a thumb-nail. The tiny creature discharges mucus from its water-jet siphon when disturbed. Oxygen in the water seems to oxydise particles of luciferin in the mucus and the flimsy cloud glows bluish-green as it expands. This continues for about five minutes and then it suddenly goes out. *Sepiola nipponensis*, another small sepioid, was found by Yata Haneda similary to discharge 'liquid fire', and Jacques-Yves Cousteau and Georges Houot, diving at 1,100 metres in the Mediterranean, discovered a 45-centimetre-long squid that produced a luminous, white, inky discharge.

Yet another function of cephalopod light organs was found in two mesopelagic squid studied by Richard Young and Frederick Mencher, of the University of Hawaii. These creatures, *Abraliopsis* and *Abralia*, undergo a diurnal vertical migration from the mesopelagic zone, deemed to be between 400 to 1,200 metres down off Hawaii, to the surface waters, sometimes less than 100 metres deep. It was found that they display different colours at different depths from photophores on their ventral surfaces, and it was proposed that in this way the squid would be camouflaged with respect to the quality of the downwelling light encountered in their daytime and night-time habitats. The colours could be altered in the laboratory by changing the temperature of the water. Colour, the researchers thought, is not significant. It is the intensity of the light that is important to provide an effective counter-illumination against detection by predators or prey. The animals, literally, eliminate their silhouette by changing the quality of the bioluminescence to match prevailing light conditions. *Abraliopsis*, for instance, is able to adjust its photophores to simulate the colour of moonlight at 20 metres below the surface of the ocean off Enewetak. The mechanism of colour change is unclear, but both bright and dim photophores have been observed in night conditions, while uniform brightness is seen at the deeper, darker, day conditions. Research is now focusing on whether the animals can exert any control over the direction of their luminescence which would further enhance their ability to match the light playing on moonlit waters.

## Ponies, midshipmen and anglers

The bony fishes, never missing an evolutionary trick, have maximised the ability to emit light in the deep sea for offence, defence, and communication.

The deep-sea angler fishes, of which there are many known species, have a light organ, known as the *esca*, on the tip of a modified first dorsal spine, the *illicium*. The spine has become separated from the rest of the dorsal fin and moved to a position at the front of the fish's head. It is pivoted at its base on a miniature ball-and-socket joint that allows the lure to be waved about in much the same way as you might use a fishing rod. The *esca* may take the form of a simple swelling or may be embellished with frills and filaments to make an appetising bait. A patch of skin without pigment allows the bioluminescence to shine through. Little predators are enticed by the movement and light and become the prey in one gulp.

The light is not produced by the fish itself but by symbiotic bacteria that are cultured in special compartments. They are encouraged to glow when oxygenated blood is pumped into their chamber. When at rest, the fish shuts down its light organ simply by cutting off the supply of blood.

The deep-sea angler *Linophryne* has a relatively short *illicium*, a frilly *esca*, and in addition, a tasselled barbel on the chin. Peter Herring of the Institute of Oceanography at Wormley, and Kjeld Hansen, of the University of Copenhagen, demonstrated that the two lures have quite different light systems. While the lure on the head is powered by bacteria, the beads of light in the barbel are produced when hydrogen peroxide comes into contact with paracrystalline granules in large glandular cells packed with mitochondria, structures associated with cell respiration. There is no nerve supply, the luminescence being apparently controlled by the blood supply.

The functions attributed to the lures of deep-sea anglers must, again, be speculative. Nobody has had a chance to watch them in their natural habitat. The shallow-water angler *Lophius*, however, *has* been studied, and has been seen to use its lighted *illicium* to lure prey towards its enormous mouth.

The black angler fish *Galatheathauma axeli*, caught 365 metres down at the bottom of the sea, has as its luminous bait a forked structure on the roof of its mouth – surely the most efficient way of catching a meal.

Viper fish *Chauliodus* behave in a similar way to the anglers. They have a modified second dorsal fin spine that has become even more elongated and can be dangled directly in front of the mouth. The fishes themselves can only be described as fearsome. They tend to be elongated, have an enormous mouth, and gigantic teeth that prevent them from closing the mouth. Fortunately they are only between 5 and 30 centimetres long.

Stomiatoid fishes, related to the viper fish, have no dorsal spines but have very long barbels under the chin. *Ultimostomias*, for example, sports a barbel ten times the length of the body. The tips of stomiatoid barbels are often equipped with light organs in the form of bulbs and streamers, and the light is produced by the glandular cell system. In addition the barbels appear to be sensitive to movements in the water. Like the anglers and the vipers, the barbel serves to lure prey.

The hatchet fish *Sternoptyx* probably attracts prey right into its mouth with the aid of two patches of luminescent tissue that can glow for up to thirty minutes at a time. The viper fish, similarly, has a bank of about 350 photophores scattered over the roof of the mouth. The lantern fish *Neoscopelus* has light organs on its tongue.

*Whip Scorpion* Mastigoproctus giganteus.

*Top:* Eleodes *(left) has chemical defensive glands.* Megasida *(right) is a headstanding mimic.*

*Bottom: Bombardier beetle* Brachinus *discharging.*

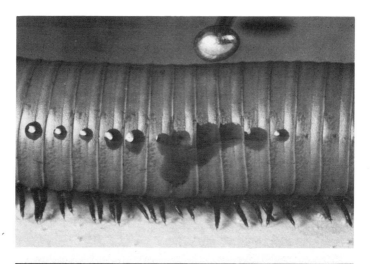

*Top: Noxious fluid oozing from pores of millipede* Narceous.

*Bottom: Rosette of sawfly larvae* Pseudoperga *emitting droplets of oily fluid from mouth after disturbance.*

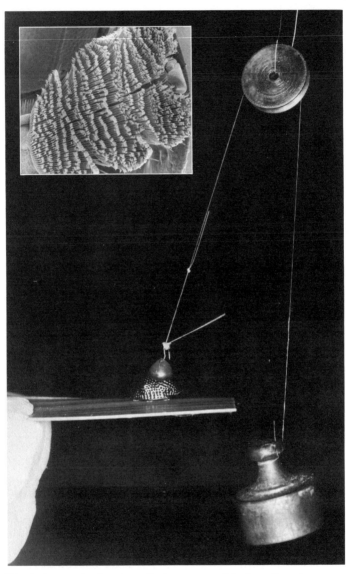

Hemisphaerota *beetle resists pull of two-gram weight. Inset: Scanning electronmicrograph of the underside of one of* Hemisphaerota's *feet.*

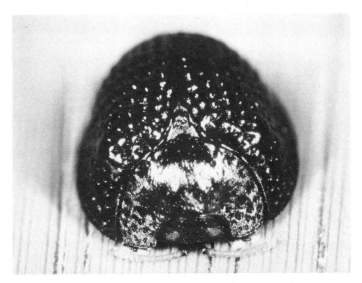

*Top:* Hemisphaerota – the beetle that won't let go.

*Bottom: Beetle larva* Cassida *with a faecal shield.*

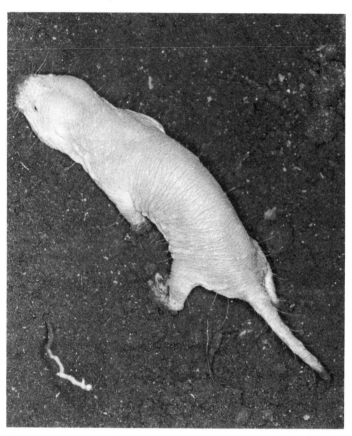

*The naked mole rat* Heterocephalus.

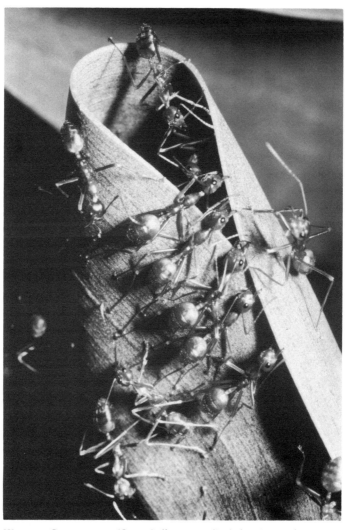

*Weaver or Green tree ants* (Oecophylla smaragdina) *drawing two leaves together for their nest.*

*Top: Male North American robin moth* Hylaphora *showing feathery antennae.*

*Bottom: Head of a male inch-worm moth with large feathery antennae.*

The marsh marigold Caltha palustris *which appears evenly yellow in normal light (top), but has patterned 'nectar guides' when seen in reflected ultra-violet light (bottom).*

*Top: Termitaria of the compass termites* Amitermes *of Australia.*
*Bottom: The flat west-pointing face of a compass termite mound.*

*Top: Nasute termite soldiers* (Trinervitermes gratiosus) *guarding a long column marching during daylight, Kenya.*

*Bottom:* Macrotermes *species, termite soldiers guarding workers, Malaysia.*

*Top: Pilot whales* Globicephala *stranded on beach.*

*Bottom: Komodo dragon* Varanus komodensis.

*Deep-sea squid* Histioteuthis *showing light organs and one eye larger than the other.*

Top: Tight clusters of giant clams, mussels and other organisms around hydrothermal vents on the Galapagos Rift.

Bottom: Pagoda-like two-metre-high mineral sulphide 'spade needle' at the Guaymas Basin taken from the deep-sea submersible Alvin (manipulator arm left). Vestimentiferan worms in foreground.

'Black-smoker' at 21° North on the East Pacific Rise.

*Waitomo Caves, New Zealand.*

Bioluminescence can also prevent a fish from becoming another's meal. Sudden flashes of light could, clearly, blind an attacker in such a way that the luminous image of the fish would be imprinted on the retina of the aggressor, enabling the potential prey to escape. William Beebe, in his book *Half a Mile Down*, recalls seeing a lantern fish *Myctophum* respond to a luminous wrist-watch by flashing its lateral light organs. Another group of fishes, the Searsidae – deep-sea herrings – produce, like squid, a luminous cloud from a gland behind the eyes.

A more subtle defence is ventral camouflage. Many deep-sea fishes, like some of the cephalopods, have their light organs pointing downwards. The hatchet fish *Argyropelecus*, for example, has all but two of its photophores directed ventrally, which would provide countershading to match the light coming from the surface and protect the animal from attacks from below. The two remaining photophores positioned just in front of, and shining into, the eyes, are thought to act as reference lights by which the fish can compare its own bioluminescence to the ambient natural light conditions. Research has further shown that the angle of the reflectors associated with the photophores also matches the glow of light from the surface, and effectively breaks up the outline of the fish from almost any angle. Pigments, in addition, filter the light being produced by the fish so that it approximates to the quality of light from above.

Many fish must seek the optimum vertical position to watch the variable light conditions from clear skies, moonlit and moonless nights, or overcast skies, but the pony fish *Leiognathus* can vary the intensity of its light and thereby gain more flexibility, yet still remain invisible. The light system of the pony fish depends on symbiotic bacteria cultivated and stored in an organ surrounding the oesophagus. The light is varied by means of a slit, the swim bladder is modified to function as an integrating sphere, and the muscle fibres serve like optical fibres to distribute the bacterially produced light along the ventral surface of the fish.

An even more extraordinary lighting system is found in the midshipman fish *Porichthys* which gains its name from the pattern of some 700 photophores, like the brass buttons on a military uniform, along its ventral surface. The light does not flash but glows. Control is thought to be hormonal, but the unusual feature is that the luciferin component of the chemiluminescent reaction is acquired in the diet from luminous shrimps *Euphausia*. In areas where the shrimps don't occur the fish are not luminous, although they still have the light organs and luciferase present.

Communication is another function of bioluminescence in fish. Flashlight fish *Photoblepharon*, which can be seen performing in the Steinhart Aquarium, San Francisco, actually flash messages at each other. The flashing is achieved, not by turning the light source on and off, but by lids that can be moved across the light organ. The organ itself is positioned directly below the eye and the lids close from top to bottom. Light is supplied by symbiotic bacteria. Flashing communication takes place between male-female pairs during inter-tidal territorial encounters, and among large shoals of 50 to 200 fish.

In addition, the flashlight fish can utilise a 'wink-and-run' strategy to escape from predators. They engage in zigzag swimming, flashing on the 'zig' and disappearing in the darkness on the 'zag', thus confusing an attacker completely. They, in turn, attract their prey of light-sensitive shrimps by switching on their pair of bright 'headlights'.

**Phantoms in the forest**
When the paratroopers landed at Arnhem in the Second World War and dug in, they were astonished to see patches of ghostly light in the ground. Closer inspection revealed the light sources to be the decaying roots of plants. Running through them were the luminescent mycelial threads of fungi. There are several fungi that are known to produce a faint, yellow-green glow, the most common being the honey fungus *Armillaria mellea*. In the First World War, soldiers in the trenches found a use for the phenomenon. They would pin a piece of rotting wood to their helmets or uniforms, and on a dark night the light was sufficient for individuals to spot each other and prevent mistaken identities. In fairy-tales and legends, the mystical wand may have had its origins in a stick glowing from luminescent fungi.

The most striking manifestation of luminescent fungi are the fruiting bodies which glow like ghosts in the forests. In the USA the Jack O'Lantern *Clitocybe* has a bluish-green hue, and in Australia the moonlight fungus *Pleurotus* gives a white light. The biochemistry and function of the steady dim glow is not known, although the luminescence of the fruiting body could have something to do with attracting insects for spore dispersal. In certain parts of Indonesia the luminous fruiting caps are worn by young girls to guide their lovers to them.

On the forest floor an animate glowing object might attract

attention. Earthworms, particularly *Diplocardia*, exude a green bioluminescent slime when attacked or prodded.

Sometimes an eerie light can be seen flying silently between the trees. It's an owl. The leading edges of its wings have become coated in a luminescent dust, known colloquially as 'fox-fire', that has come from the luminescent fungi growing around the entrance to its nest-hole.

## The Waitomo illuminations

Hanging from the roof of the Waitomo Caves in New Zealand are hundreds of luminous strands that form a bright, luminescent curtain. They are made by the larvae of the dipteran fly *Arachnocampa luminosa*, and they are the way that this enterprising insect catches its food. The larvae themselves cling to the ceiling and exude sticky threads that can be seen in the dark. Prey insects, attracted by the light, are caught and trapped on the strands, reeled in like fish on fishing lines, and then eaten. A single larvae may drop as many as seventy threads at a time.

## Femmes fatales

Over 3000 years ago Chinese poets waxed lyrical about the light of the firefly. Aristotle joined them, recognising things that 'give light in the dark'. Shakespeare, on the other hand, was singularly unimpressed with the glow-worms 'uneffectual fire', but he hadn't seen the sight that greeted the Spanish conquistadors in the West Indies, who saw the native peoples using the click beetle *Pyrophorus* as a source of illumination in homes, and as an item of adornment in their hair or on their clothes.

Glow-worms and fireflies are not worms or flies at all, but beetles. Their luminosity is an aid to courtship. The female European glow-worm *Lampyris*, for instance, is flightless, looks like a larva, glows in the dark, and attracts the male towards her. He has a very faint light organ that appears to serve no function. North American fireflies, however, flash at each other. Male *Photinus pyralis* fireflies flit on an undulating course just 50 centimetres above the ground, drop down every 5.8 seconds and give a half-second flash. Any female within two metres will wait two seconds and flash back. Each species of firefly has its own Morse code. *Photinus consimilis* males have slow flashes, delivered in groups of three when the insect is 3 or 4 metres from the ground. *Photinus granulatus*, swoops near to the ground and bounces from side to side, whereas *Photinus consanguineus* has a flash pattern of two short flashes two seconds apart, repeated every five seconds.

By matching flashes the fireflies find mates of their own species. Some fireflies, though, deliberately set out to break the code.

At the University of Florida in Gainesville, James Lloyd and Steven Wing swung light-emitting diodes in the air and noticed that they were attractive to female *Photuris* fireflies. The attraction was not for mating, though; the *Photuris* females *attacked* the flashing diode. They would home in on their prey like 'sidewinder' missiles. Further research revealed that during courtship the *Photuris* females synchronised their flashing with the *Photuris* males flying overhead, and encouraged them down to mate. But they would also mimic the flashing code of *Photina* males and entice them down to their deaths. *Photuris* females deceive *Photina* males, eat them up, and gain extra nutrients for egg-laying. A cunning tale, but there was yet more to tell. Re-enter Tom Eisner of Cornell University.

Female fireflies are vulnerable to predators when seeking a place to lay eggs. Wolf spiders and ants are common predators. *Photina* females, however, are relatively safe, for they have poisonous steroids in their blood. *Photuris* females don't. These *'femmes fatales'* acquire their supply from the *Photinus* males.

Evolution, though, is 'catching up' with *Photuris*, for the researchers have noticed that American fireflies behave differently to those in other parts of the world.

In two species, the males give a quick flash and drop to the ground, rather than fly directly to the flashing female; just in case. And, in one species, the males have given up flashing altogether, relying instead on chemical attraction.

As for the poison, there is another facet to the story, as Tom Eisner found when he made use of a new microscopic technique, known as scanning electron micrography (SEM). Put simply, it allows an observer to examine a microscopic object from almost any angle. It can also literally freeze a piece of behaviour. Eisner froze the act of an ant attacking a firefly and examined it in detail.

He found that if a firefly is caught napping by an ant and the ant attacks by biting into the firefly's body, the beetle exudes blood. The SEM showed that the blood oozed out, not at the site of the injury, but from minute pores along the beetle's carapace. In the blood is a solution that will paralyse the ant's jaws and make the attacker back away.

Other researchers have found the firefly beetle's poison to be so powerful that when offered to, say, Atlantic sharp-nose sharks *Rhizoprionodon terraenovae* it causes instant paralysis.

Tom Eisner and Jerrold Meinwald found *Photinus* poisons to

be made up of lucibufagins, chemicals that affect the heart of vertebrates. The closest chemical relatives are the bufadieno-lides found in certain toads, and which are some of the deadliest poisons known to man.

## A flash in the dark

Fireflies that flash in the middle of the night emit light of a different quality to those that flash at dusk. In order to be seen clearly against the background mosaic of leaves and twigs, *Photinus consanguineus, Photinus macdermotti* and *Photinus collustarans* produce a yellow-coloured light, an adaptation to make the signal stand out at dusk. *Photinus ignitus* and *Photinus tanytoxus*, the late flashers, produce a green light. Some fireflies of the same species, found in different habitats, such as those in Florida swamps and Maryland woods, emit different coloured lights at various times of day according to the light conditions.

The males of some species in Asia and the Pacific regions gather in trees and flash in synchrony. Hugh Smith, an American naturalist encountered the phenomenon when travelling in Thailand. 'Imagine a tree', he wrote, 'with a firefly on every leaf and all the fireflies flashing in perfect unison. . . . Imagine a tenth of a mile of river-front with an unbroken line of trees with fireflies on every leaf flashing in synchronism . . . if one's imagination is sufficiently vivid, he may form some conception of this amazing spectacle.' Scientists were intrigued to know how the fireflies keep in step.

The light organ in the abdomen is triggered to flash by signals emanating from the insect's brain. Stimulation of the eye results in the production of a flash. The time taken for the eye to perceive the stimulus, transmit to the brain, process the signals, generate motor impulses, transmit them down the main nerve cord and out through the peripheral nerves to the light organ, and then excite the organ to produce its light, takes about 200 milliseconds. If synchronous fireflies flashed every 200 milliseconds then an explanation for synchronisation would be simple. Inconveniently, they do not. The most common synchronous firefly in Thailand, *Pteroptyx malaccae*, has been found to flash every 560 milliseconds and another, *Pteroptyx cribellata* from New Guinea, every second, and they never get more than 20 milliseconds out of step. Individuals must be responding to each other's flashes of light, and so some sort of pacemaker must be intervening to keep the speed of delivery of the signals species-specific. Experiments by members of the

*Alpha Helix* expedition to New Guinea, led by John Buck, of the National Institutes of Health, showed that not only is there a network of cells forming a pacemaker but that it can also be reset, and the whole mechanism works much like the charge-discharge system in stroboscopes. Why, though, should fireflies want to keep in step? What advantage is to be gained?

John and Elizabeth Buck came up with a suggestion. In jungle areas, uninterrupted communication between males and females trying to locate each other would be impossible because of the density of the foliage. A large flashing beacon would be easier to spot, as an insect, homing-in on the tree, zigzags between the branches and leaves in the forest.

Unfortunately this 'altruistic' explanation does not tally with the fact, put forward by James Lloyd, that mutant individuals circumventing the flashing system could 'cheat', thereby getting the choice females and breeding the need to flash in synchrony out of the species.

There is, however, evidence that the 'flashing trees' are permanent. Local river peoples are known to use the trees as navigation beacons, and local naturalists have studied the same community of fireflies for periods of up to five years. This has led Lloyd to suggest that the fireflies are arranged in 'leks', with one female subjected to the amorous intentions of a cluster of males. For physiological reasons, the males flash their courtship signal together. If they flashed out of synchrony the chances are that they would be flashing when the female is in that 200-millisecond period after having responded to a flash, processed the signal, and taken action. During that short period she would be unreceptive to any flashes of light. Indeed, work with North American fireflies has shown that the female may be desensitised for several hundred milliseconds after receiving a light flash. In addition, the female would find it easier to compare flashes that are received simultaneously, and thus it would be to the advantage of the male to flash with his neighbour, but be that little bit brighter to gain a mate.

## A torch for medicine

Little is understood, at a fundamental level, about the way chemical energy, upon which all life depends, is converted, say, into electrical energy for nerves to work. Bioluminescence may help us to find out, for it involves a basic process by which chemical energy is converted into light energy. The process might also provide medical researchers with a probe by which they can examine chemical activities within the cell. If the substances involved in bioluminescence can be introduced into a cell, for instance, every time an energy conversion process takes place, and adenosinetriphosphate (ATP) is released, a flash of light could be detected. By monitoring the flashes, the medical observer could monitor activity inside the living cell without affecting its normal working. One application has been seen already in anaesthetics.

On 16 October 1846 at the Massachusetts General Hospital W. T. G. Morton used ether as an anaesthetic in an operation carried out by J. C. Warren. A hundred and thirty-eight years later we still do not understand the precise way in which anaesthetics work inside the cell. Bioluminescent bacteria, it has been found, dim in the presence of anaesthetics, and in direct proportion to the potency of the particular anaesthetic in man.

Bioluminescence is already being employed clinically. Kits are available containing firefly luciferin and luciferase that can be used to measure accurately the amount of ATP in a cell. Apparently it is a million times more sensitive than any other method and is being routinely used in testing for signs of heart disease.

The study of bioluminescence, although seemingly quite trivial at first, is beginning to make important contributions to the study of a fundamental process in biology and in medical research.

# Individual Labels

A few years after the Revolution a surviving French aristocrat, hiding in his chateau in Lorraine, placed a copper ring on the leg of a swallow. For three years he watched the bird and its mate return to the same nest site. This was the first reliable account of a bird having been ringed and studied. A hundred years later, in 1899, the Danish naturalist, Christian Mortenson, ringed 164 starlings with identifiable rings so that each bird had its own individual label. Today we use satellites in space, radio-telemetry, coloured dyes, plastic tags and a host of other techno-logical marvels to tag animals on the move. The eighteenth-century copper ring and the twentieth-century radio transmitter, though, have one important thing in common – they allow a scientist to follow an individual animal during its everyday life, with the minimum of interference, revealing where it goes and why it should want to go there.

## Bird ringing

In 1555 Olaus Magnus, the Archbishop of Uppsala in Sweden, announced to the civilised world that swallows spend the winter months hibernating underwater rolled up in a tight ball. A fisherman had told him so. The scientific community believed him. Linnaeus swallowed the tale; John Reinhold Forster, in 1735, claimed to have seen them being dragged up from a river; Baron Cuvier was convinced that they were at the bottom of the marsh; and Geoffrey de St Hilaire, in 1772, thought he saw them sleeping. Daines Barrington went into print in that learned journal, the *Philosophical Transactions of the Royal Society*, and bullied all the naturalists of the time into believing that swallows hibernated in winter. The dissenters had been ignored.

In the fourth century BC the Greek poet Anacreon suggested that swallows overwinter on the banks of the Nile, migrating back to Europe each spring. Frederick II of Germany, who lived between 1194 and 1250, recognised that birds move from north to south when the cold weather comes in autumn.

In 1678 Francis Willughby suggested that swallows fly to hot countries like Egypt and Ethiopia, and Gilbert White, in 1767, recorded his belief that they fly south to avoid the bad winter weather. Unfortunately, White came under the influence of Barrington and unwisely went along with the hibernation hypothesis.

George Edwards and John Hunter could not stomach Barrington's preposterous ideas and said so. Edwards, in the mid-1700s wrote: 'It is enough to raise one's indignation, to see so many vouchers from so many assertors of this foolish and erroneous conjecture, which is not only repugnant to reason, but to all known laws of nature.' Hunter went further and carried out a series of experiments. Swallows, he found, could not survive underwater, and indeed, they had absolutely no desire to enter water when given the opportunity to do so. The immersion theory and hibernation hypothesis, however, did not go away until the mid-nineteenth century. In 1824 it has been recorded that Edward Jenner spoke out against it. It was not until bird-ringing became more widely used as a method of tracking the movements of birds that the underwater nonsense was finally scotched. Bird-ringing schemes are now global. The British Trust for Ornithology, for example, rings upwards of half a million birds of many species each year and gets back about 12,000 recoveries from all over the world. The migrations that ringing has revealed are remarkable.

Swallows from the British Isles, for example, spend the winter in southern Africa. Each spring they head north across the Sahara desert, the Mediterranean, and western Europe to breed. Most of the journey can be achieved in short bursts, but the leg across the Sahara must be done in one long flight without food and water. On the southern shores of the Mediterranean the swallows can be picked off with ease as they rest there completely exhausted. When the swallows eventually reach their destinations they are among the first aerial feeders to arrive each spring. It is likely that in the distant past swallows lived in the Southern Hemisphere for the entire year, since their flying insect prey is not available in the north during the winter months. When the swallow population enlarged in southern Africa, individuals would have moved gradually northwards to breed, finding less competition for food and longer daylight hours in which to catch it. Today over 200 million swallows are in the mass exodus.

All the European swallows overwinter in Africa, while those

from north-eastern Asia find their way south to India, south-east Asia and occasionally into northern Australia. Those nesting in Germany do not overwinter so far south as the British and Russian birds. They set off from central Africa each spring, saving some 5,000 kilometres on the round trip.

Ringing has shown that many species of birds make incredible journeys. The arctic warbler *Phylloscopus borealis*, while having its main population in central Asia, is found to fly back and forth from northern Norway to south-east Asia. The wheatear *Oenanthe oenanthe* spends its winter season just south of the Sahara. From there, two main populations have been heading progressively further north to nest and breed. The north-western group have found Britain, the Faroes, Iceland and Greenland, and are heading into north-eastern Canada. The north-eastern group have traversed eastern Asia and have spread across the Bering Strait into north-western Canada. At the most northerly part of their summer range the two populations are about 800 kilometres apart.

But, perhaps, the world record for distance covered must go to a sea bird, the arctic tern *Sterna paradisaea*. Those birds that live in the far north, such as Spitzbergen, are known to fly the furthest south. Some individuals make an annual round trip of 40,000 kilometres, flying, literally, to where the sun never sets. Before they are even six months old, the young terns will have left their nest site in the Arctic and flown south to moulting sites inside the Antarctic Circle. In the first few years of life, they circumnavigate the South Pole, following the icy cold and stormy Southern Ocean, until the urge to reproduce once more pulls them northwards along the west coast of Africa and Europe, up the east coast of the British Isles, and once more on to the breeding-grounds deep inside the Arctic Circle. Curiously, those breeding further south do not fly so far. Farne Islands birds, for example, pitch up on the South African coast during the boreal winter, sampling the pickings in the nutrient-rich upwellings of the cold Benguella current.

## Shark tagging

The sports fishermen of the north-east United States and Canada have been taking part in an exciting and sometimes dangerous scientific experiment. They have been tagging some of the most ferocious sharks in the sea. Sports fishing in North America is a very popular sport and it occurred to Jack Casey, a fisheries biologist from the North East Fisheries Center of the National Oceanic and Atmospheric Administration, at Narragansett, Rhode Island, that weekend fisherman have the best opportunity to tag and release a large number of sharks.

The Apex Predator Task, which includes the co-operative tagging programme, is aimed at providing information primarily on stock management. Until recently very little was known about the numbers and distribution of sharks in the north Atlantic, and the US National Marine Fisheries Service was becoming aware that this resource was commercially important both to sports and high seas fishing interests. With 250,000 sharks being landed every year, it was clear that some figures were needed so that management strategies ensure the availability of these resources in the future. The study, which also includes tuna, billfish and swordfish, has the added advantage of not only revealing information about the resource but also providing basic scientific understanding of sharks themselves with on-going research on migration, age, growth, food and reproductive habits.

The co-operative tagging programme has been running for over twenty years, during which time about 50,000 sharks and other predators at the apex of their food chain have been tagged by 2500 sports fishermen, commercial fishermen and scientists. A tag consists of a little plastic capsule containing the individual's number and returning instructions. It is attached to the shark with a small barbed dart. A stainless steel needle on a long pole is used to thrust the dart into the muscle at the base of the large dorsal fin. The message in the capsule is in English, Spanish, French, Norwegian and Japanese. So far the longest capture-release-recapture time has been seventeen years and the greatest distances recorded are in excess of 5000 kilometres. Blue sharks have been showing the most remarkable journeys.

Blue sharks, *Prionace glauca*, are probably the most numerous of the large oceanic sharks. They are sleek, with long snouts and characteristic sickle-shaped pectoral fins. Large specimens can reach 4 metres in length. Individuals that were tagged in the New York Bight have been recaptured across the Atlantic, along the coasts of Europe, off the Cape Verde Islands, in the Caribbean, and off the north-east coast of South America. Blue sharks tagged around the Canary Islands have been recaptured off the coast of French Guiana and Surinam. One specimen has been found to cross the equator. What was even more interesting was the distribution of males and females.

Large male blue sharks have only been caught off the Atlantic seaboard of North America, whereas females are found on both sides of the ocean. There seems to be a gigantic migration cycle that moves in a clockwise direction, following the currents of the North Atlantic Gyre, but only the female blues follow it. The mating-grounds appear to be in an area off southern New England, but why the females should travel the North Atlantic is a puzzle. With large males as potential cannibals, could it be that the females move elsewhere to give birth? Could it also be that when Europe and the Americas were closer together the females didn't move so far, and that the present journey is the product of continental drift? (See Chapter 7.) We shall have to wait and see the results of future work.

Another aspect of the shark-tagging programme is the pattern of arrivals along the North American Atlantic coast during the early summer months. Just as the spring migration of birds is linked with weather fronts and temperature patterns, so too is the northward migration of sharks dependent on temperature variations in the sea. There are sharks that swim ahead of the warm isotherms and those that follow. First to arrive are the blue sharks. Those that have not headed off to the eastern Atlantic overwinter in deep water, off the continental shelf of North America or in the Sargasso Sea. In May they move northward over the continental shelf and into the coastal waters near Cape Hateras, probably in order to mate, although fertilisation itself occurs elsewhere, for the females store the sperm from the summer mating until the following spring. The inshore movement in spring is generally in front of the 20°C isotherm. Blue sharks prefer the cooler water. Behind, in the slightly warmer water of late June, come the mako sharks, *Isurus oxyrinchus*, and the swordfish, *Xiphias gladius*. And, in mid-July, still warmer water marks the arrival of the tiger sharks, *Galeocerdo cuvieri*, and hammerheads, *Sphyrna* spp. Further south, in the warm seas off Florida, these species of shark can be found all the year round, but in the temperate waters off southern New England there is this seasonal movement.

At the nearby Woods Hole Oceanographic Institution, another group of researchers has been experimenting with radio tags on large sharks and have come up with some extraordinary findings. Traditionally, we think of fishes as cold-blooded creatures, their body temperatures depending on the surrounding sea-water temperature. Some species of sharks and tuna, it seems, can regulate their temperature, keeping their powerful swimming muscles a few degrees warmer, and therefore more efficient. The blood vessels that serve these muscles, so dissection has revealed, look a little like a heat-exchanger that prevents body heat from being carried off by the circulating blood and lost at places, such as the gills, where the vascular system has close contact with the outside sea water. Radio tags attached to probes that can detect temperature changes in swimming sharks, have sent back signals to scientists following in boats. These show that the muscles are kept at 7–10°C above the ambient temperature of the sea. Physiologists have shown that for every 10°C rise in muscle temperature there is a threefold increase in muscle power.

It is quite significant that the three sharks showing this heat-retention system are some of the most powerful fish in the sea – the great white shark *Carcharodon carcharias*, otherwise known as 'the man-eater', which is the largest known predatory fish; the mako shark, which often leaps clear of the water when hooked by a sports fisherman; and the porbeagle *Lamna nasus* which is often caught off the south Cornish coast.

## Radio wolves

Many animals, from snails to elephants, have been fitted with radio transmitters and tracked. Numbered rings and tags only give an observer information about the release and recapture point of a creature's movements. Radio tracking fills in some of the gaps. An animal can be given its own signal and followed either with a portable, hand-held receiver in the field, or an array of strategically placed stations can automatically keep tabs on its every move. Transmitters have been 'glued' to the backs of tortoises, implanted beneath the skin of ducks, worn as harnesses by penguins, and harpooned into the blubber of whales, but perhaps the most frequently used method for mammals is the radio collar that fits loosely around the neck of the subject. It appears not to irritate the animal wearing it, and thus it does not interfere with its everyday life. Pandas, foxes and wolves have been fitted with radio collars. We still know little about the life of pandas and foxes, but we *have* made considerable progress in understanding the life of the wolf, in particular the timber wolves of North America.

Imagine the scene. It is very early in the morning. In the half-light four timber wolves stalk a small group of white-tailed deer. The pack leader creeps gingerly towards one particular individual, which by some unknown and invisible signal has betrayed itself as weaker than the rest. The herd spots the pack and makes off. In a short burst of speed the wolves reach and tackle their prey, bite at the stomach and legs and bring the creature down. In seconds it is all over.

The carcass lies on the forest floor, but the wolves do not begin to eat it at once. First, they raise their heads to the brightening winter sky, and howl.

Far in the distance a neighbouring pack replies. Ravens passing overhead veer sharply, doubling back in a searching zigzag flight to investigate the commotion. They hover briefly over gaps in the forest canopy, eventually swooping down to perch on the trees around the site of the kill.

Hidden nearby and watching this dawn performance are zoologists with radio-tracking equipment. One wolf has a radio collar that transmits signals to a direction-finding receiver, and the zoologists, first from a light aircraft and then on foot, have been following the pack as it scours its territory for prey through Minnesota's Superior National Forest.

Wolves often howl after a kill. This ceremony is not for the benefit of scavenging birds or curious scientists, but is a piece of social behaviour about which we have very little understanding. We can guess at some of its possible functions, and researchers like L. David Mech, of US Fish and Wildlife Service, and Fred Harrington, of Mount Saint Vincent University in Halifax, Nova Scotia, have been doing just that, with information gathered from field studies undertaken in the past couple of decades.

'A wolf pack', says Harrington, 'is nothing more than a family group, and social relationships are very positive within that group.'

An explanation for the howling is that during the chase animals are separated from the main pack and, in their way, are distressed. They want to return to the group, and the howling ceremony provides an audible beacon. Individual identities might be contained in each wolf's howl. A 'roll-call' may ensure that all the pack are present and safe before the feast begins.

'Each pack, though', suggests Harrington, 'is a separate social entity, and relationships between packs are very hostile.' Apart from man the hunter, the animals most likely to be dangerous to wolves are other wolves. Packs are careful to avoid contact with each other. 'In Minnesota, the number-one cause of adult wolf mortality is being attacked and killed by other packs.' Howling, then, can also be a form of long-distance proclamation, spacing packs at safe distances and ensuring that they avoid physical confrontation which could be damaging to both parties.

Howling is particularly important when a pack finds itself at the edge of its territory, which does not have distinct boundaries. Each pack ranges over an area of 80 to 400 square kilometres, surrounded by a kilometre-wide strip in which it could encounter its neighbours. If a pack is in this zone it is of mutual advantage to indicate to rivals that it is there, and to keep clear.

But the only precise and long-lasting way of advertising territorial rights involves another of the wolf's senses – smell. 'Scent-marking,' says David Mech, 'certainly is at least as important to a wolf as is howling.' Usually it is the adults highest in the social hierarchy that carry out the marking. During their travels across the centre of the territory they mark every three minutes, which means that an olfactory signal is posted about every 150 metres. Within a kilometre of the edge they double up, so if the neighbours are going through that strip too, there are four times as many marks on the boundary as in the centre of the territory.

Territorial declarations, it seems, are made in complementary advertisements. The howl tells a neighbouring pack what the residents are doing at any given moment, but a howl does not last, whereas the scent mark may be good for two to four weeks, depending on the weather. It will tell neighbours, not where the resident pack is but where it has been, and what area it claims.

A wolf pack in Minnesota usually consists of one or two parents, their cubs and several other adult wolves. Packs today tend to be smaller than in the past because game is scarce, but in Alaska packs are still seen with up to twenty adults. Each pack has a dominant, or 'alpha' pair and, as the male is often larger and stronger, he usually takes the role of pack leader. Members of the pack are subservient to the alpha male, and only when another dares challenge his position is there discord.

In a social group such as a wolf pack, communication between individuals is important to maintain the integrity of the pack, to attain status, and to facilitate pack activities. In wolves, communication involves all the senses.

There is, for example, a complex visual language. In *The Expression of the Emotions in Animals and Man*, published in 1872, Charles Darwin noted that in dogs (the domestic version of the wolf, after all) an aggressive animal will make itself appear large by stretching its legs, erecting its ears and raising the hair at the back of its neck. A friendly or submissive one will make itself appear small, with ears flat and tail wagging or between the legs. To these, add the gamut of facial expressions like the baring of teeth, body movements, postures and attitudes such as tail-wagging and submissive rolling over, and a complicated visual body language is revealed. Coat and muzzle contact allows tactile communication. Eric Zimen, of West Germany's Universitat des Saarlandes, recorded the average muzzle-to-muzzle or muzzle-to-coat contact rate between a group of travelling wolves to be six per wolf per hour, the dominant animals and the cubs making the most contact.

The wolf's sense of smell is important for signalling both between individuals and between packs. Urination may pass messages between pack members as a kind of group bond, and in the mating period information about the state of readiness of the female to mate may be contained in her urine. At the Edinburgh Wolf Symposium in 1978, David Mech put it succinctly: 'Wolves that pee together stay together.'

Besides scent-marking with squirts of urine, wolves are sometimes seen depositing faeces on stones, bushes or tree-stumps. When fresh, the smell is strong, and faeces several days old may still warrant attention from inquisitive trespassers. And then there are the mysteries. What purpose is served by the two anal glands, and the gland at the base of the tail? Why do wolves – and dogs, come to that – wallow in material giving off pungent odours? Are they disguising their own smells for purposes of olfactory camouflage during hunting, or for some reason are they doing the opposite – enhancing their scents? Or do they just enjoy it?

Sound communication is not limited to howling. Wolves have been variously attributed with barks, growls, squeaks, whines, whimpers, songs, snarls, yelps, yips, yaps, growl-barks, bark-howls and any further combination you can think of. Paul Joslin of the Chicago Zoological Society settled for four categories of vocalisation – bark, growl, whimper and howl.

The short, explosive bark appears to draw attention to the vocalising animal. It contains a broad range of frequencies and its harshness makes it easy to locate. Animals are often in a conspicuous position when barking. In some circumstances it is possibly a challenge or warning – a kind of 'who goes there?' – in response to a disturbance such as an intruding bear or human, and sometimes the bark might be a decoy, for instance, to distract a rival or predator away from cubs. Barks often mark the end of a howling session.

The deep growl seems to be a warning signal or threat, and a precursor to an attack. Adults also growl to subdue or restrict the behaviour of cubs; a female will growl to dissuade cubs from attempting to nurse. A growl-bark is often heard when danger threatens the well-being of cubs, and when it is given, cubs head rapidly for the den. In general the growl appears to be a signal to put distance between individuals – either social distance in the pack hierarchy or physical distance during pack activities.

Whimpers are high-pitched, close-range, positive-contact sounds. They have a variety of functions quite the opposite of the growl. Females whine to encourage cubs out of the den. When hungry or in pain, pups solicit attention from adults with a whimper. A subordinate adult whimpers to a dominant one as an approaching and greeting display. A sexually receptive female may whimper.

Rudolf Schenkel, who observed the behaviour of wolves in Basle Zoo, recalls one particular female trotting along 'with springing dance steps' while 'tenderly singing'. It is interesting to speculate that, when more advanced analyses and behaviour studies are carried out, wolf signals that sound more or less alike might turn out to be quite distinct and have different meanings, much like the vervet monkeys' grunts and alarm calls. When these were analysed by Dorothy Cheney and Robert Seyfarth they were shown to represent objects and events in the outside world – much as words do in human language.

Howling can be spontaneous. At morning and in the evening, one wolf will start and, after two or three howls, the others will join in. The howls are long at first, gradually working up to a chorus of high, short bursts. The group howl can last, on average, between a minute and a minute and a half, and can be heard as far away as 8 or 10 kilometres. It is a long-distance signal, and it increases as the mating season approaches and again when pups are about. Pups start to howl quite early, at two months, having developed the sound from a whimper.

Each wolf establishes its own status and has specific duties that benefit the entire group. The young and the strong hunt, while the old and the injured guard the home ground and the cubs. Often a pack has a core of efficient hunters led by the alpha pair and some of their oldest offspring. Others sometimes go along for the ride, occasionally slipping in at the kill for a nip but staying well clear if the prey is as large and as dangerous as a moose.

New packs are created when splitting takes place. If the number of animals in a pack grows too large for the hunting territory to support, the newly matured wolves, along with older animals and perhaps some juveniles, might move off or be seen off, banished to a distant territory. On the other hand, an abundance of food could mean a wolf population adjusting to prey availability and splitting, in a kind of expansive phase.

A subordinate member, anywhere between ten months and four years old, would begin to break its ties with the main pack and forage along the edge of the main territory. Here it would be in the territorial buffer zone of neighbouring packs, the advantage being that the edges of territories are frequented less than the centres by the main residents.

Subordinate members of the opposite sex from other packs are also likely to be breaking away, and a liaison might be made. If the two animals are compatible and courtship is successful, then they begin scent-marking and howling, gradually carving out their own, albeit smaller, territory. Successful breeding and the raising of cubs appear to give the new pair confidence, and they assert themselves more in establishing their home ground. This results in compression of other pack territories.

The 'lone wolf' represents a third method of dispersal. In this case a single animal will wander around the territories of many packs, sometimes covering as much as 500,000 hectares searching for an area as yet unpopulated by wolves, or a segment of a large territory rarely visited by the resident pack. Here again, the lone wolf must chance upon an available mate before it can colonise its own patch of land.

In the winter months the female of an established pack goes into oestrus, and it is she who leads the group as it wanders, often in single file, about its territory. For about a fortnight the alpha male follows her tail closely, guarding his position and her flank against the advances of the other males in the pack. The second-ranking male usually follows at a discreet 5 metres behind the alpha pair. Low-ranking females are not allowed to mate, and any subordinate pair caught copulating will be attacked by the rest of the pack.

As the alpha pair mate, the sounds most commonly heard are the whines or whimpers and the growls. As he courts, the male utters high chirp-like squeaks. Fred Harrington once witnessed an alpha male giving the most extraordinary high-pitched utterances for about fifteen minutes before copulation. 'The sound had a ventriloqual effect. Although you knew the male was producing it, it seemed as if it was coming from everywhere.' If the female is unimpressed she rebuffs the male with growls. If a subordinate male approaches, the alpha male will snarl and growl a warning, to put him firmly in his place. After mating, the alpha male often loses interest in the female, does not stay as close to her and thus allows some of the younger males to copulate with her.

Nine weeks after mating the nomadic pattern of the pack ceases. From spring to autumn its activities are focused around 'home sites', where the cubs are born and reared. In late April or early May, the alpha female retires to the darkness of the den and gives birth to three or four blind and naked pups. They stay inside for three weeks, nursed by the mother, and are eventually encouraged to emerge only by her whimperings outside the entrance.

For a month to six weeks, before the pups are weaned, the pack remains in the vicinity of the den. The young adults go out each day to hunt but return to this fixed site, sometimes with and sometimes without prey. When the youngsters are able to travel, the pack moves away from the den, and journeys between 'rendezvous sites', which may be changed several times during the summer.

The developing cubs are restricted to the immediate vicinity of the den while the adults radiate out in search of food. They later return, stomachs filled with 5 to 10 kilograms of food, some of which might be regurgitated to the cubs. The pups elicit this feeding reaction by jumping up and nuzzling the adult's muzzle. The regurgitation thus stimulated appears to be almost uncontrollable. Fred Harrington has watched pups mob returning adults, which have then regurgitated and re-eaten their regurgitate as if they really didn't intend to give the food but couldn't stop the reflex once the pups had started it.

If the mother joins the hunting party and is away too long, the youngsters begin to howl. This long-distance call becomes a close-range whimper as the mother approaches. If the cubs get too boisterous, pulling the mother's ears and tail, she will scold with a low, soft growl.

The feeding of the cubs may not be restricted to the parents, for co-operation is well developed in wolf packs. Pup-raising is a collective activity. The elder brothers and sisters of the current litter will feed the pups, care for them and protect them from marauding predators such as bears or other wolves.

In September when the pups are five or six months old, they join the hunting adults, and gradually the pack becomes nomadic again, travelling perhaps 50 kilometres a day from kill to kill. The hunt is usually preceded by a group howl accompanied by much nuzzling, nose-pushing and greeting. The howl may be a way of locating a neighbouring pack and, if there is an answer, the wolves know which area to avoid. Or, if the rivals are too close to the home site, it might be worthwhile chasing them out.

As they move the wolves attempt to catch any prey animal they find but they are not, it seems, as clever at this as was once thought. They make many attempts for each success. In one study David Mech found that a pack, on average, might chase twelve or thirteen moose or deer for every one brought down and killed. A healthy moose is likely to stand its ground, and the wolves will back off. A deer between two and five years old is well able to outpace a wolf pack.

The young and infirm animals are the most vulnerable, and wolves, Fred Harrington has observed, are adept at spotting the best targets. 'In some cases you'll see them chase a deer for several miles, whereas in other cases they'll give up after a hundred yards. There must be something that the deer is communicating, unconsciously, by its running behaviour, that tells whether it is catchable or not.'

When wolves kill they do it in a different way from the big cats. Lions, for example, tend to strangle or suffocate their prey. A wolf does not have a killing bite, and so the strategy is to dodge in and tear at a bit of the animal, often directing the attack to the rear with bites at the belly or the flanks. When the prey can no longer keep going, the pack will pile in and tear the animal apart.

Wolves sometimes tackle large animals like moose. Here they need to be extremely careful, for a moose's front hooves are formidable. Indeed, a direct hit could kill a wolf. In this case one wolf will go for the moose's nose, grab it and hang on for dear life. The front end of the moose is then immobilised, and the rest of the pack will come in from the rear and bring the animal down.

When the moose is dead there is another 'howling ceremony'. Stragglers come in to feed, and youngsters with their guardians and the older pack members catch up.

If food is abundant, the pack may leave a considerable amount of meat behind – fair game for the scavengers. 'Raven in Minnesota', Harrington discovered, 'depend on carrion during the winter, and much of this comes from wolf kills.' The birds locate their next meal by listening for the group howl.

If food is scarce the pack will eat almost everything of the kill. An animal too large for one sitting will be put in cold storage, as it were, and finished off at a later date.

When times are hard, wolves go scavenging too, occasionally turning up at rubbish dumps alongside bears. Fights between wolves and bears are usually avoided, although occasionally one will chase off the other. David Mech remembers one wolf pack that he was radio tracking encountering a female bear in her winter quarters. 'The wolves pulled the hibernating bear and her two cubs out of the den and killed them. To our embarrassment, it turned out that the adult bear also had a radio collar and was being studied by someone else.'

## Polar bears from satellites

The polar bear *Ursus maritimus* is the symbol of the Arctic, but until quite recently its lifestyle has been a complete mystery. It was thought at one time that bears sit on ice-flows and drift clockwise around the North Pole, obligatory boreal nomads, at the mercy of the currents and eddies of the drifting ice, eking out an existence from their sterile environment. Long-range tracking experiments have shown that this is quite wrong.

Polar bears, it appears, live in large familiar areas. They may travel considerable distances, indeed, telemetric tracking from satellites in space has shown that an individual can walk 40 kilometres a day for many days. Alaskan bears that are for some reason larger on average than other bears, can cover twice that distance per day. They can also travel against the direction of ice drift. About three-quarters of the ice in the polar basin pours out between Svarlbard and Greenland into the Greenland Sea, sweeping down the east Greenland coast at a drift rate of about 25 kilometres a day. The bears on this flow, it has been found, can walk against the drift and accurately navigate back to their home bases.

Polar bears in different areas have acquired different skills. Svarlbard bears eat mostly seals, whereas the Hudson Bay bears have taken up a lifestyle similar to the brown bears, with dens in the forest and a summer diet of berries and birds. This is interesting in that it marks a regression to an ancient way of life. It is thought that the polar bear and the brown bear *Ursus arctos* had a common ancestor, the Pleistocene bear *Ursus etruscus*, and have only evolved into the two species we see today during the last 20,000 years. No fossil remains of polar bears have been found in deposits that were laid down before the last Ice Age. The predominantly carnivorous habit of the polar bear is thought to be a relatively modern adaptation to life in the Arctic. Some Canadian bears have developed a novel way of catching seals by swimming under them. The Svarlbard bears have not evolved the same hunting method, preferring to wait by an air-hole or creep up on a victim and swat it dead with one blow of the powerful forepaw.

Female polar bears spend much of the winter months in a den, consisting of a cave on land or a depression in the snow on the ice-flows, in which she has the season's cubs, usually twins. One pregnant female, in 1977, was responsible for a period of East-West co-operation. Equipped with a radio transmitter that was being tracked from a US satellite, the bear crossed the Bering Strait from Alaska and began to wander about in Siberia.

A great deal of the polar bear biology that has been revealed in the last ten years has come from researchers working from a small town in Manitoba which just happens to be on the bears' seasonal migration route. Churchill has become known as the polar bear capital of the world. Local inhabitants wear sweat-shirts that proclaim 'Our Household Pests are Polar Bears'. Every autumn the bears arrive in large numbers and the town must take appropriate action. Focus of attention is the garbage dump. It appears that dominant animals have staked out spheres of influence along the shores of Hudson Bay, and the less powerful have been left with the area that includes the town. Ironically, the underlings get the choice morsels from the town's garbage.

When the ice breaks up in early summer the polar bears arrive on the shore. They move in to a 26,000-hectar area behind the coast where the dens of the females are to be found. As the first chill of winter comes, the males travel back to the coast, passing through Churchill *en route*. Snacks at the town dump tide them over until they are able to go hunting once more for their pre-ferred prey – the ringed and bearded seals of the Arctic seas.

The bears are tracked, tranquillised, and fitted with radio transmitters. Radio collars are not used any more as they fall off too easily. Instead, the scientists implant a miniature transmitter near the bear's ear. Each bear also acquires its own identification lettering painted on to the white fur in water-resistant dyes. The researchers have already found that the bears visiting Churchill each year are regulars. They constitute a population of about 200 animals that move about in this particular area. So far, only one Churchill bear has been found wandering elsewhere, and one individual flown 650 kilometres away and released back into the wild returned to the study area within a few weeks, after having swum considerable distances.

## Sharks from space

On 27 June 1982 a 7-tonne basking shark became the first fish to broadcast from a satellite. It was the climax of a five-year experiment aimed at developing a satellite tracking system for large marine creatures. Heading the research team at the University of Aberdeen has been Monty Priede, and it is his opinion that the system they have developed could be used with whales in order to track their migrations and their numbers. It could even be used to spot illegal whaling.

The basking shark, the second largest species of fish in the world, is an interesting creature to study for so little is known about its life. Many grow to 9 metres and weigh up to 7 tonnes. The largest on record was 13.7 metres long. The basking shark feeds on plankton which it filters from the surface waters by swimming slowly along, propelled by its enormous upright tail. The mouth gapes open some 80 centimetres and rows of gill rakers can sieve 1500 tonnes of water per hour giving the shark about 2 kilograms of shrimps, mostly copepod crustaceans from the drifting zooplankton.

Most of the information related to basking sharks comes from observations of the animals in summer months when they can be seen literally basking at the surface. They are common off the west coast of Scotland, although they were once commoner, but became victims of the shark-fishing industry in that area. Today they are pursued by scientists. Little is known about the way they reproduce, for instance. In 1936, however, a Norwegian fisherman was reported to have caught a large female and was towing it back to harbour when it gave birth to six 1.5-metre-long babies. Of all the sharks that have been caught that was the only pregnant female. Where the rest are hiding is a mystery. Another complete mystery is where they spend the winter.

Folklore tells us that basking sharks head off to Morocco for the winter. This species is, indeed, found off the coast of Africa and in other tropical waters but that may simply be a reflection of the worldwide distribution. Off Scotland, sharks have been caught in deep water during the winter so could they be hibernating there? There is some evidence to suggest that these sharks shed their gill rakers and lie dormant on the bottom of the sea unable to feed from autumn to spring. They grow new gill rakers each year. Priede's tracking system has been designed to try to solve the mystery.

The transmitter is placed on a small floating platform shaped like a torpedo. A tow-line is attached to the shark by a harpoon.

One of the biggest problems has been to get the harpoon to stick. On one occasion a flip of the tail of one of these gigantic creatures overturned the research dinghy and spilled all the scientists into the water. When the line is finally secured the transmitter functions only at the surface. If the shark dives deep the platform can be towed below, whereupon the transmitter switches itself off. When they return to the surface, the transmitter switches itself back on again. After a few months a 'weak-link' in the tow-line breaks and the shark is free once more.

During the 1982 experiment, the shark towed the transmitter for about seventeen days, but the 'weak-link' proved to be too weak and broke too early. However, the system was proved to be effective. Radio signals at 400 megahertz were beamed to the NOAA-7 satellite and other polar-orbiting satellites carrying Service Argos radio-location equipment. The coded signals were relayed to a ground station dish at Toulouse and the data telexed to Aberdeen. In this way about sixteen fixes a day were obtained on the shark's position. During the short experimental period the shark stayed in-shore, scooping up the masses of plankton that could also be spotted from the satellite. Infra-red and colour photographs of the sea around the shark were an added bonus, giving information about the surface temperatures and the distribution of the phytoplankton on which the small crustacean zooplankton feed. Unfortunately, the premature breakage of the 'weak-link' meant that the scientists were unable to follow the shark during the crucial autumn months, and so the basking shark's lost winter is still a complete mystery.

# Continents on the Move

The theory of continental drift and the principles of plate tectonics caused a revolution in the geological sciences comparable to the impact Darwin's theory of evolution had on biology. The theory had an uncomfortable ride for over 100 years before becoming acceptable to the scientific community. As is often the case, the pioneers were long since dead before their contributions to the story could be recognised for what they were. It was, after all, difficult to throw contemporary scientific thinking aside and ask geologists to accept that the continents move, when there was very little evidence to suggest that they did, let alone any mechanism to cause it to happen.

Nevertheless, when the theory was written into the textbooks, it not only had a profound effect on geophysical thinking, but also allowed biologists to understand the movement and distribution of certain extant and extinct plant and animal communities.

## Continental drift – the human history

The nineteenth-century American geologist, A. Snider-Pellegrini, was fascinated by the way in which the eastern seaboard of South American and the west coast of Africa fitted like a jigsaw. He proposed that once they were joined, being broken apart at the time of the biblical Flood. Working in Paris in 1858 he published his hypothesis in *La Creation et ses Mystères Devoiles*, but it had all the impact of a damp squib. Two hundred years before, in his *Novanum Organum* of 1620, Francis Bacon had thought it 'no mere accidental occurrence' that the coastal outlines of the Old and New Worlds on either side of the Atlantic bore some resemblance, and the Frenchman, Francois Placet, wrote in 1658: *'La corruption du grand et petit monde, ou il est montré que devant le deluge, l'Amerique n'etait point separée des autres partie du monde.'* Theologian, Theodor Lilienthal, also turned to the Bible for an explanation in 1756, to be followed by the explorer, Baron Alexander von Humboldt who, in 1800, drew attention to the similarities in the shores of the east and west Atlantic, but likewise attributed the separation of Africa and South America to the Flood.

But, the scientific community of the nineteenth-century was not to be moved. The orthodoxy of the day stated that the continents were static, fixed in their present positions since the earth first took shape. The earth, it was suggested, was simply contracting to produce earth movements. Mountain building, for example, was likened to the crinkling of an apple skin when the fruit dries and shrinks. A few biologists, with Darwin's new theory of evolution fresh in their minds, had their doubts about the establishment view. Remarkably similar fossil plants and animals were being found on the opposite sides of deep ocean basins. J. H. Pepper, for instance, had found identical fossil plants in coal measures in both Europe and North America. Without former land-bridges, why were the fossils not strikingly different, as one might expect of isolated populations?

It was not a biologist or a geologist, however, who spoke out against establishment geology. It fell to the German astronomer and meteorologist, Alfred Wegener, to challenge the existing theories. He wasn't the first. Two American geophysicists, Frank Taylor in 1908, and Howard Baker in 1911, independently put forward the notion that the continents have moved across the earth's surface, but their voices were unheard. Wegener's was.

At a lecture in Frankfurt in 1912, Wegener stood up and announced his revolutionary new idea – the theory of continental drift. His initial motivation was climatological. Somehow he needed to explain how tropical ferns could have grown in Greenland. But his evidence was drawn from many scientific disciplines. In 1915 many of his papers were brought together into a book, *Die Entstehung der Kontinente und Ozeane*. Wegener proposed a gigantic single continent, about 275 million years ago, that he called Pangea, meaning all earth or all land, and it was surrounded by an ocean, called, not surprisingly, Panthalassa or all sea. It split into two super-continents – Laurasia, in the north and Gondwanaland in the south. Gradually, during the past 180 million years, these two land masses broke up, the pieces moving to their present positions as the continents of the world.

The book was translated into English in 1924 as *The Origin of Continents and Oceans*, and international debate became heated. Wegener lost his scientific respectability and had a hard time finding a job. He eventually obtained a teaching post at the

University of Graz in Austria. He had few supporters. Alexander du Toit and Henno Martin searched Africa and Brazil for evidence, but little was heard about the theory until the 1930s when Arthur Holme, of the University of Edinburgh, proposed convection currents, driven by the earth's internal radioactive heat, as a possible mechanism for continental movements. The Dutch geophysicist, F. A. Vening Meinesz, suggested that the continents moved like giant icebergs across the molten mantle of the earth. But it was not for another thirty years, in the 1960s, that the theory gained universal respectability and a tangible mechanism was proposed.

Harry Hess, of Princeton University, became interested in the topographical features that were being found at the bottom of the Atlantic Ocean. There were mountains and valleys just as on the continental surfaces, and the thickness of the underlying mantle was found to be much thinner than that under the continents.

The major feature in the Atlantic seemed to be a chain of under-sea volcanic mountains running down the middle of the ocean. It became known as the Mid-Atlantic Ridge. Hess proposed that magma, from deep down, welled up at the Ridge and gradually spread eastwards and westwards. This sea-floor spreading, he suggested, was responsible for the continents of Africa and South America moving apart. Fred Vine and Drummond Matthews, of the University of Cambridge, found that this model could be tested by looking at the magnetic properties of the rocks in the sea floor.

When molten lava cools to about 450°C the earth's magnetic field influences the minerals in such a way that when the rock is laid down it contains a magnetic memory of the geomagnetic conditions at the time. The ocean floor is like a piece of magnetic tape, recording each geomagnetic reversal in the earth's history. By following the series of reversals across the sea floor, symmetrical patterns were found on either side of the Mid-Atlantic Ridge. This supported Hess's model, and moreover provided a rate of spread. Africa is moving away from South America at about 2 centimetres a year. This meant, however, that in view of the known age of the earth, there should be more ocean floor than we can actually see. It seemed unlikely that the earth was expanding, so where did it go? Hess had already proposed that it is destroyed, maybe at the deep-ocean trenches. Later, several workers came up with the idea that ocean floor dives down into the mantle, and at these subduction zones there is likely to be volcanic and other seismic activity.

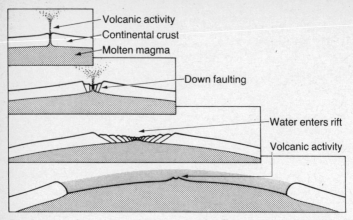

*Development of an ocean and mid-ocean ridge (bottom picture shows flooded rift).*

In 1967 British geophysicist Dan McKenzie, together with R. L. Parker, introduced the world to *plate tectonics*. Their classic paper, published in *Nature*, brought together all the theories, observations, and speculations on continental drift and sea-floor spreading, and proposed that the earth's surface is divided into a series of moving plates with each continent sitting on its own plate. The following year Princeton geophysicist Jason Morgan worked out a world map of tectonic plates.

Attention then focused on the seams between the plates. The Mid-Atlantic Ridge is, in fact, a double row of volcanic peaks, between which opens a long crack in the earth where molten lava from the mantle is exuded. It is known as a constructive plate margin, giving rise to the African plate to the east and the South American plate to the west. Iceland, which sits astride the Mid-Atlantic Ridge, is in consequence getting a few centimetres wider each year.

Plates are destroyed at the destructive plate margins or subduction zones. The western edge of the Pacific plate for example, meets the Asian plate and dives below it, to be recycled by the convection currents in the fluid mantle below. Subduction zones are also characterised by volcanic and seismic activity, but, in contrast to the oozing black basaltic furnaces of the mid-oceanic ridges, these volcanoes are explosive. Krakatoa, for example, on the line of weakness (an island arc) between the Indo-Australian plate moving north and the south-east Asia section of the enormous Eurasian plate, was witness to that. In 1883 it literally

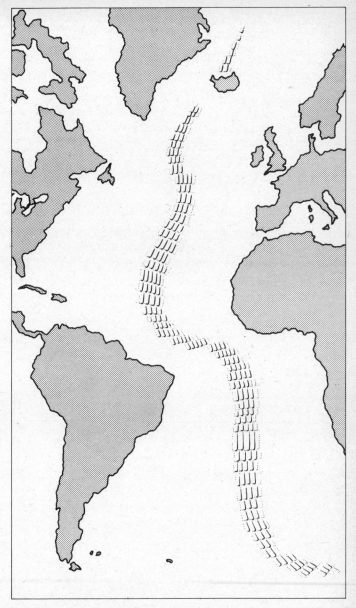

*Floor of the Atlantic Ocean showing mid-ocean ridge. Through such ridges the new oceanic crust is generated.*

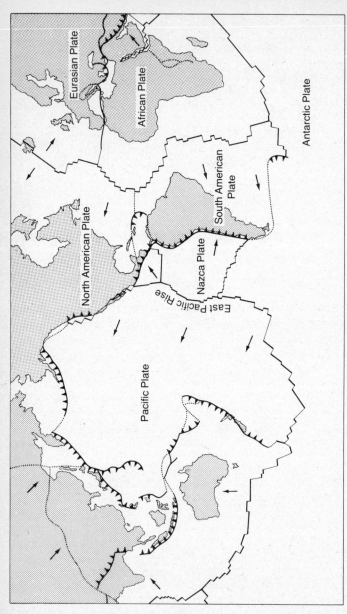

Major plates of the Earth's crust and the directions in which they are moving. Dotted lines show probable plate margins, arrowheads destructive plate margins with underthrusting in the direction of arrowheads

blew itself apart in the biggest bang in the earth's history. The explosions were heard at Alice Springs in Australia – about 3000 kilometres away; night came for twenty-four hours to neighbouring islands and the mainland, and dust in the upper atmosphere circled the earth for years giving some of the amazing skies and sunsets that were recorded by the brush of contemporary artists. In more recent years, the eruption of Mount St Helens, in the north-western United States, was a product of the activity associated with the Pacific plate diving below the North American plate. In one enormous event the mountain blew its top off, the blast ejecting millions of tonnes of rock and sediment in a sideways explosion.

Perhaps the most important contribution of plate tectonics was to give us a drifting jigsaw puzzle which indicated the areas of the earth most likely to be subjected to catastrophic volcanic eruptions and earthquakes. Most seismic activity is associated with plate margins, and so it is here that scientists have been able to focus their attention in an attempt to predict major events accurately; but that's another story.

## Continental drift – the natural history
### Permian
Imagine all the continents being squeezed into one enormous megacontinent. This was how Pangea was probably formed, about 250 million years ago, when Laurasia, the continent of North America, Greenland and western Europe; Angaraland, with Siberia, China and Korea; and Gondwanaland, with India, Africa, South America, Australia, and Antarctica, were pushed together by encircling ocean plates. Uplifting caused Pangea to be the largest continent without a sea that there has ever been in the earth's history.

Antarctica was placed, as it is today, over the planet's south pole, and the rest of southern Gondwanaland suffered glaciation. Laurasia, northern Gondwanaland and southern Angaraland consisted of hot, dry deserts, while northern Angaraland was a warm and humid area.

Ferns and conifers were locally common. In the seas, the ammonites nearly died out; on land, insects were diversifying rapidly. Reptiles were racing ahead of the amphibians for terrestrial supremacy. *Dimetrodon*, a 3-metre-long predatory pelycosaur, ruled the roost. It had a large sail on its back, perhaps to pick up the rays of the morning sun and warm the creature ahead of its rivals – a distinct advantage. The pelycosaurs were the forerunners of the mammal-like reptiles, including a cunning nocturnal line of therapsids that outlived the dinosaurs and eventually gave rise to the mammals. Fossils of a small fish-eating reptile, *Mesosaurus*, found both in southern Africa and Brazil, encouraged Wegener to compile his theory. Similarly, fossils of a seed fern, *Glossopteris* were found in South America, Africa and India, and used as supportive evidence.

## Triassic

For about 80 million years Pangea changed very little. In the sea the bivalve molluscs took over from the ammonites as the most diverse group of marine invertebrates. Dinosaurs filled every ecological niche open to them on land and to a certain extent at sea. Conifers, ferns, cycads and ginkgos – the gymnosperms or naked seed plants – dominated the flora.

## Jurassic

About 170 million years ago, Pangea started to break into two super-continents – Laurasia in the north, and Gondwanaland in the south. A rift valley appeared at the sites of the present-day Atlantic and Indian oceans. India split away from Africa and was pushed north towards Asia. North America moved away from north-western Africa. The polar ice-caps disappeared, and temperate conditions were experienced in the Arctic and Antarctic. The equatorial tropical zone was likely to have been much broader than it is today.

Giant reptiles, like the long-necked *Brontosaurus*, *Diplodocus*, and the armour-plated *Stegosaurus* roamed the warmer parts of the earth. *Archaeopteryx*, one of the first birds, began to fly. The dolphin-like ichthyosaurs and the Loch Ness monster-like plesiosaurs swam in the sea. Turtles and crocodiles appeared on the scene. Mammals were very small and insignificant. The ammonites recovered and diversified once again. Gymnosperm forests covered the land.

## Cretaceous

About 135 million years ago the North Atlantic and Indian ocean rifts filled with water to become seas. Australia and Antarctica separated from Africa and South America. India was about 3000 kilometres from Asia but still heading north. Africa swivelled anticlockwise to butt against Asia, and pulled the Iberian peninsula with it to form the Bay of Biscay. There was a surge of sea-floor spreading and a subsequent rise in sea level. Land that had not been submerged since Pre-cambrian times went below the waves. The Sahara was then a sea. The climate was generally warm.

The flowering plants appeared, ousting the gymnosperms, and forests began to be dominated by broad-leaved deciduous trees. *Pteranodon*, the giant-winged reptile soared in the skies. Giant 4-metre turtles and 10-metre plesiosaurs lived in the sea, and giant herbivores, like *Iguanodon*, the horned *Triceratops*, and the largest terrestrial carnivore ever known to have lived – 15-metre-high *Tyrannosaurus* – walked the continents.

About 110 million years ago a rift developed between Africa and South America. Later this area flooded and the South Atlantic Ocean was formed about 80 million years ago.

*Tertiary*
About 64 million years ago the dinosaurs and many other living things, including ammonites, belemnites and a host of plank-tonic marine organisms, died out. The climate throughout the world cooled. The North and South Atlantic were respectively about 95 per cent and 75 per cent of their present-day width. London enjoyed a sub-tropical climate. It was the start of the 'Age of Mammals'.

About 50 million years ago Greenland split from Scandinavia, and the mammal faunas in Europe and North America became isolated as a result of the break in the land-bridge. The Pyrenees began to be pushed up between France and Spain. Glaciation appeared in the Antarctic.

About 38 million years ago the Antarctic iced over and the thermal structure of the oceans, as we find it today, was formed.

About 30 million years ago Australia and New Zealand bid farewell to Antarctica, allowing the circum-Antarctic Current to flow and mix the waters of all the oceans. In warmer climes, pig-like mammals and rhinoceros appeared. Elephants and whales were getting larger. Rodents, carnivores, and a variety of herbivorous mammals were diversifying. The Bering land-bridge still allowed the migration of animals between Asia and North America.

About 18 million years ago Africa bumped into Europe, pushed up the Alps, and trapped the Mediterranean Sea. African elephants, cattle and pigs took advantage of the join and ventured into Europe. India collided with Asia and thrust up the Himalayas. Terrestrial mammals peaked in size, with the giant 5-metre-high *Deinotherium*, an unusual elephant that lived in

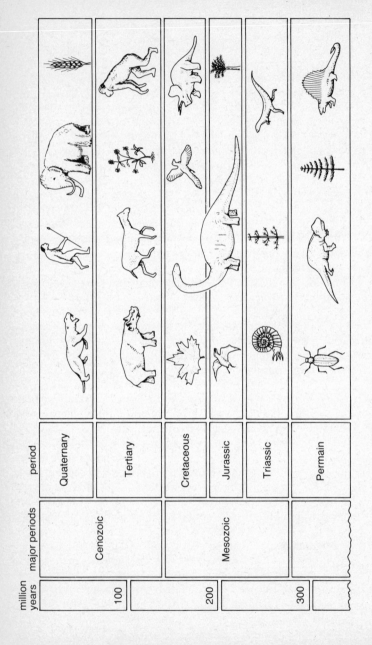

| period | major periods | million years |
|---|---|---|
| Quaternary | Cenozoic | 100 |
| Tertiary | | |
| Cretaceous | Mesozoic | 200 |
| Jurassic | | |
| Triassic | | 300 |
| Permain | | |

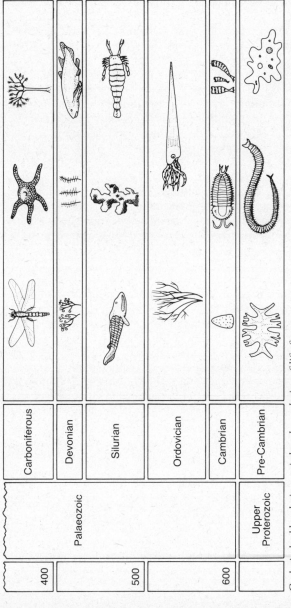

| | | | | | | | |
|---|---|---|---|---|---|---|---|
| | Carboniferous | | | | | | |
| 400 | Devonian | Palaeozoic | | | | | |
| | Silurian | | | | | | |
| 500 | Ordovician | | | | | | |
| | Cambrian | | | | | | |
| 600 | Pre-Cambrian | Upper Proterozoic | | | | | |

*Geological table relating period to the evolution of life-forms.*

Africa, and the four-tusked mastodons. Deer and pigs lived in oak forests. Monkeys appeared, and so did antelopes and early giraffes. Horses were well on the way to evolving their modern size and shape, migrating from North America, via the Bering land-bridge to Asia.

About 7 million years ago the Straits of Gibraltar opened, followed, about 3.5 million years later, by an uplift at the isthmus of Panama. The Atlantic and the Pacific oceans became separated for the first time in 125 million years, but the bridge became a busy highway for migrating mammals. Horses, tapiers and llamas went south, while sloths and armadillos travelled north.

Man was emerging in Africa.

## Observations from space

Until recently it has been difficult actually to measure the continents moving. Monitoring the movements across faults or at places where continents are touching, such as the zone where the Indian subcontinent is squashing against Eurasia along the line of the Himalayas, has tended to be unreliable. Now astronomy and space science have come to the rescue and NASA's crustal dynamics project run from the Goddard Space Flight Center has developed two methods of measuring continental movements.

One method involves several radio telescopes, located on different continents, focusing on sources of light way outside our own galaxy and known as quasars. With a clever bit of trigonometry the distances between the telescopes can be accurately obtained. In this way the continent of Europe has been found to be moving away from North America at a rate of 1.3 centimetres a year.

Another method uses satellites orbiting the earth. Laser beams from ground stations are bounced back to earth off reflectors on the satellites and the time taken for the event is measured. With a figure for the speed of light and another equation the distance can once more be measured. With the help of a ground station in Hawaii, it has been found that the Pacific plate is moving away from North America at a rate of 4 centimetres a year, while Australia, which sits on the Indian plate, is moving towards Hawaii at 7 centimetres a year.

Along the San Andreas fault in California, the two sides of the fault have been sliding relative to each other at about 6 centimetres a year for the past eleven years.

## Continental rafts

Southern beeches, *Nothogagus* spp., grow on the western slopes of the Chilean Andes. One deciduous species, the Nire or Guindo *N. antarctica*, to be found on Navarino Island of Tierra del Fuego, grows nearer to the Antarctic than any other tree. A closely related evergreen species *N. solandri* constitutes the black beech forests of New Zealand, together with silver, red, hard and mountain beeches. The tangle-beech *N. gunni* turns up in Tasmania, and the myrtle beech *N. cunninghamii* in south-east Australia. Another thirteen species are found in New Guinea, together with another five on New Caledonia. Indeed, a total of thirty-six southern beech species are found exclusively in isolated populations in South America and Australasia. Their fruits are poor dispersers, ruling out ocean currents and birds for long-distance travel. How did they each get to the places where we find them today?

Southern beeches, it seems, have a long history. Fossils have been extracted from Cretaceous rocks that were laid down about 100 million years ago, but these specimens were found in the Antarctic. Here was the clue, for 100 million years ago the Antarctic was part of the Gondwanaland super-continent, along with South America and Australia. When Gondwanaland split into its constituent continents, the various populations of beeches were rafted to their present positions.

The same was probably true of the hoop pines *Aracauria* spp., with the monkey puzzle tree or Chile pine on the western slopes of the Andes, the parana pine or candelabra tree of Argentina, the bunya-bunya of Queensland, the Norfolk Island Pine, the New Caledonia Pine and the Moreton Bay Pine of Queensland and New Guinea.

Leptodactylid frogs, migadopine, carabid and ground beetles and peloridiid bugs are similarly dispersed. But perhaps the most intriguing of the isolated communities are the marsupials, a group of pouched mammals with names like koala, bandicoot, wombat, Tasmanian devil, sugar glider and kangaroo.

There are about 250 known species of marsupials living to-day, and they are to be found in North and South America, New Guinea, and Australia. In evolutionary terms, they have 'converged' on the same basic body forms, and filled the same ecological niches in Australia, for instance, that the rest of the 4200 placental mammal species do in the other parts of the world. The marsupial sugar glider parallels the North American placental flying squirrel, for example, and the marsupial mole resembles the South African golden mole, to the extent of sharing the habit of 'sand-swimming'. The Tasmanian wolf or thylacine, which might now be extinct (although, as I write, naturalists with the latest tracking equipment and automatic cameras are trying to find any remaining individuals), lives in a similar manner to the North American timber wolf.

One of the fundamental questions is where did the marsupials originate? One suggestion is that they first developed in North America, during the Cretaceous period, and migrated across South America and a much warmer Antarctica to Australasia, all of which were joined at the time as Gondwanaland. An alternative hypothesis starts them off in South America, with a few migrations north.

A vast number of species are represented in the fossil record of South America. The earliest, at 100 million years old, are insectivore-like creatures that evolved from the early shrew-like pantothere mammals. It is thought that they probably represent part of the ancestral stock which gave rise to the rest of the marsupials. There were marsupial dogs and hyenas, and sabre-toothed marsupials, playing the same ecological role as their placental counterparts in North America and Europe. About 50 million years ago a few migrated to western Europe, following the land-bridge that then existed across the Arctic circle, but they were extinct 40 million years later.

Australia's marsupial fauna was thought to have arrived much later, about 25 million years ago, suggesting a migration from South America. The oldest fossil so far recovered is about 23 million years old, but the rich diversity is not seen in the sediments until 15 million years before the present, when enormous lion-like thylacoleoids, with tusk-like incisors and shearing molars, were found alongside marsupial rhinoceros, and a 3-metre-tall kangaroo.

And, that was the story until they found a fossil flea in 100-million-year-old deposits in Victoria. Its biting mouth parts, according to Michael Archer, of the University of New South Wales, were eminently suited to annoy mammals, but of the mammals themselves not a tooth has been found.

Another puzzle is that no placental mammals have made the same move to Australia. Could it be that Australia is the marsupial source? A migration in the opposite direction, from Australia, via the Antarctic and northward into the Americas is the alternative hypothesis put forward by John Kirsch, of Yale University. This would mean marsupials competing successfully with the placental mammals for ecological niches. Until now, the presumption had been that the marsupials were inferior to the placentals. This theory would certainly turn the tables. Hugh Tyndale-Biscoe, of the Australia National University at Canberra, goes even further in suggesting that both the placentals and the marsupials had a global distribution and fought it out, in an evolutionary sense, to fill the available niches.

No matter which theory of migration holds up, we must turn again to continental drift for an explanation of the isolated population. Having established themselves in South America and Australia, the marsupials were most likely rafted to their present positions after the super-continent – Gondwanaland – was broken apart. But was there any evidence for all this? The key discovery would be fossil marsupials in the Antarctic. None were found until 7 March 1982, when Sankar Chatterjee, of Texas Tech University, uncovered the jaws and teeth of a squirrel-like polydolopid in rocks estimated to be 40 million years old on Seymour Island, off the coast of the Antarctic peninsular. It was the first mammalian find in Antarctica, and the first real evidence that the marsupials of South America and Australia could have been moving between the two continents, via Antarctica, prior to 56 million years ago. It still did not resolve, however, in which way they were heading, although the leader of the expedition, William Zinsmeister, of Ohio State University, proposed that the migration was from South America *to* Australia. Unfortunately the lack of fossil-hunting activity in Australia until quite recently has meant that the question must remain, for the present, unresolved.

And if that is not enough in the way of antipodean puzzles, why are there no marsupials on New Caledonia and New Zealand? Indeed, how could these islands have acquired Gondwanaland trees, with their accompanying insects, without the vertebrates that would have been lying in them and on them?

### 'Artefacts of the Devil'

Trilobites found on both sides of the Atlantic have been offered as evidence of both the squeezing together of Pangea and its subsequent break up. Fossils estimated to be 400 to 500 million years old were found in North and South Carolina. Two species of the genus *Paradoxides*, for example, were found on the east coast of the USA and exactly matched trilobites found in Europe and Africa. Similar finds have been made in 450-million-year-old deposits further to the north, in New England and Canada, where trilobites, similar to those unearthed in Britain, were discovered.

In 1966 Tuzo Wilson of Toronto University proposed that the sediments containing these fossils were laid down many hundreds of millions of years ago on *opposite* sides of a great ocean. As the continents were pushed together into the megacontinent, Pangea, the sediments were thrust up and wrinkled to form the Appalachian Mountains, now barely a suggestion of their former size. The continents split leaving a slice of Europe and Africa behind. The study of strata in Scotland and Scandinavia has been used to demonstrate that a chunk of America similarly headed off with Europe at the time of the separation.

Further work has suggested that the trilobites were living near an island-arc of volcanoes, similar to the Aleutian Islands today. They would have been located off the coast of Europe and Africa before Pangea was formed. They are now thought to be represented by the Slate Belts of the Carolinas along the east coast of the USA.

## Hawaiian pioneers

How did such a diversity of animals and plants reach the remote and seemingly inaccessible Hawaiian island chain, isolated as it is in the middle of the Pacific Ocean? Have the species drifted on ocean currents, or been blown by the wind? Were there landbridges that we can no longer see, or continents that were once on the doorstep but have now drifted away? Biogeographers once argued violently about the relative contributions of each of these factors, but just recently, with the acceptance of continental drift as a workable hypothesis, both drift and dispersal are considered together in order to find an explanation of the islands' colonisation.

Many of the 2500-kilometre chain of islands are still active volcanoes, the oldest and smallest islands in the west and the youngest and largest in the east, and they have never been connected to any of the continents. The nearest land is Johnston Island, about 1000 kilometres to the south-west. Yet, Hawaii has received plants and animals from many of the lands bordering the Pacific (the so-called 'ring-of-fire', on account of the profusion of volcanoes). The hardy pioneering plants came from the Indo-Pacific region to the west. Before man arrived, there were thick hardwood forests of great koa, ohia lehua, and Hawaiian sandalwood. Their seeds probably drifted singly across the ocean, or in rafts of matted vegetation containing grasses and shrubs. Sometimes islets of drifting plants, with trees rising several metres into the air, have confused passing mariners. On board may be insects and spiders, lizards and snakes. Hawaii, though, had no native amphibian, and no mammals before man, except for a solitary species of bat.

Most of the birds of Hawaii seem to have flown in from the Americas to the west or the Asian mainland to the north-east. The ne-ne looks like a descendant of the Canada goose, albeit with longer legs and reduced webbing on the feet, and lives on mountainsides rather than beside water. And similarly, the Hawaiian duck is probably a relative of the North American mallard. Storms and unfavourable winds may have blown them off course to be deposited on these remote islands. The eggs and young of snails and insects may have been encased in mud around their legs.

The ancestry of some Hawaiian plants and animals is unclear. One of the strangest plants is the silversword, one of thirteen species of mountain plants that occur nowhere else in the world. The silversword starts as a dense cluster of sword-like, silvery leaves in the dry cinders of a volcanic crater, but after twenty or so years sends up an enormous flowering stalk, and then dies. Tarweeds in Chile may be the link.

On Hawaii there are several textbook examples of what is known as adaptive radiation, the changes which occur as a species evolves characteristics which differ from the development of the main stock elsewhere, or which make it better suited to a particular niche. On the island of Oahu, for example, each of five adjacent valleys has its own species of snail that evolved from a common ancestor.

Honeycreepers, probably from tropical South America, have surpassed Darwin's Galapagos finches for diversity. There are narrow-billed nectar feeders, broad-billed seed eaters; those with bills for tearing into fleshy fruits and even a surrogate woodpecker.

But, perhaps the most interesting creatures in the context of our story are the Hawaiian fruit-flies, *Drosophila* spp. There are hundreds of species now living on the islands, and their ancestry is well worked out. Fruit-flies have 'giant' chromosomes that allow biologists to read their genetic code, and establish their lineage. For example, twenty-six species of large picture-winged fruit-flies are endemic to Big Island (Hawaii), the largest and youngest island at just 700,000 years old. Their nearest relatives on the older islands, Maui (1.8 million years old), Oahu (3.3 million), and Kauai (5.6 million) have been identified, and it was reasoned that the tiny flies island-hopped, with flushes of adaptive radiation on each, until they reached the end of the chain. It has been calculated that as few as twenty-two inter-island colonisations, over a period of 6 million years, would account for speciation observed.

But, biochemical dating indicates that Hawaiian fruit-flies diverged from their pioneering relatives from the mainland at a date estimated to be between 15 and 42 million years ago, long before the oldest Hawaiian island emerged from below the sea. How can that be? The answer, it seems, is in plate tectonics.

The Pacific plate, which underlies most of the Pacific Ocean, is being formed at a spreading centre under the west coast of North America and the south-eastern Pacific. The plate is moving slowly westwards, where it meets and dives below the Eurasian plate. In the centre of the Pacific plate there is an area of local volcanic activity, known as a volcanic hot spot. It is miles from any active plate boundary, but it is directly below the Hawaiian islands chain, and indeed is the reason for the islands being there at all. As the plate moves over the hot spot, new islands are thrown up and added to the chain, the latest being the volcanically active Big Island.

The rest of the chain gradually moves westwards away from the hot spot and area of uplift, eventually becoming inactive and sinking below the surface of the sea. The tiny Hawaiian low islands (11 to 27 million years old) and the submerged Emperor seamounts (37 to 70 million years old), to the west of the Hawaiian chain, are probably the remains of the islands on which the ancestral flies landed 40 million years or so ago.

### The legless lizards of Baja

The worm lizard *Bipes* of Mexico is an odd little creature. It has two legs at the anterior end and a long worm-like body. It spends the best part of its life underground, using its feet as shovels to excavate tunnels. The lizard only surfaces after the rains when the burrows are flooded. Favourite places are near tree roots where beetle larvae, termites and other insect prey are to be found.

There are three species, all closely related, but found in three quite separate places. Two species live near Acapulco, on the Mexican mainland, while the other is found on the Baja peninsula. Rafting or swimming across the Gulf of California have been rejected as possible dispersal mechanisms, as has a migration around the top of the Gulf. How then did the populations become separated?

Baja, it seems, has been moving to the north and to the west since 15 million years ago. The spreading centre, which gives rise to the Pacific plate, is in fact under the American west coast. All the land on the western side of the centre is separating from the American continent and heading north-west. Most of California, for example, is likely to split away from the USA along the San Andreas fault and end up next to Alaska. Baja has already split from Mexico and, although still attached at its northern end, is also heading in the same direction. The 23-centimetre-long worm lizards have been rafting away, continental fashion, with the land mass on which they live. The populations have been split and have evolved into distinct species.

Further earth movements in the form of mountain-building, which pushed up the Sierra Madre del Sur, divided the mainland population again, resulting in the three species we see today.

## The green sea turtle mystery

At the time of the dinosaurs, about 100 million years ago, a group of marine reptiles began to appear that were to become the green sea turtles. It is a curious success story, for at each stage of a green turtle's life, it is subjected to every hazard that nature can throw at it; crabs, lizards and sea birds pick off the young on the beach, and tiger sharks are particularly fond of turtle meat in the sea. Nevertheless, green sea turtles outlived their dinosaur cousins and are still with us after these millions of years – man permitting, that is.

The green sea turtles *Chelonia mydas* of Brazil are a curiosity amongst migrating sea turtles, for they travel over 2000 kilometres and find a 90-square-kilometre island in an 80-million square-kilometre ocean, simply to lay their eggs. Why do they make this incredible journey, and how do they find their way?

Ascension Island is a minute dot in the middle of the south Atlantic Ocean. It sits midway between Africa and South America on the Mid-Atlantic ridge, and is about 2200 kilometres upstream from the north-east coast of Brazil in the unyielding westward-flowing Equatorial Current. Today, the island is the stopping-off place for British servicemen heading for the Falklands. During the Second World War, the Ascension Island refuelling post, for US aircraft on the way to South-East Asia, became a legendary navigational hazard. If a pilot missed the island, it meant ditching, probably never to be seen again, in this notoriously stormy part of the Atlantic Ocean. Green turtles from Brazil not only find the island, but return to the exact same beach over which they had scuttled, as hatchlings, many years before.

The Equatorial Current brushes past numerous protected bays along the Brazilian coast. Here, fields of marine grasses provide ample food for green turtles. With their horny, serrated beaks they chomp at the roots of sea grasses and the fronds of seaweed, bolting their food without chewing. Well-nourished individuals can grow to the size of large round coffee-tables; adults weigh up to 230 or 280 kilograms.

Along the same stretch of coast there are more open and exposed, but predator-free, surf beaches, ideal for sea turtle egg-laying. But the green turtles do not lay their eggs here. Instead, they travel 2000 kilometres across the sea, against the powerful ocean current, to the beaches of Ascension. They locate the island with a navigational skill that puts man's twentieth-century navigational technology in the shade and, swimming at a rate of about 50 kilometres a day, they reach their goal in nine to ten weeks; and all this probably without food.

The green turtle's entire life history is quite a mystery in itself. Nothing is known about the turtle hatchlings' formative years at sea, for example. They just disappear. The distribution of adult males is virtually unknown, and, for several key parts of their lives, the females are out of contact. Archie Carr, the doyen of sea turtle research, and his colleagues at the University of Florida have tried to unravel the green turtle mystery. They speculate that turtles have a migration circuit composed of three essential elements – sandy beaches for egg-laying, nursery areas yet to be discovered, and feeding-grounds. Adult females, for instance, seem to have a two to three-year circuit when they migrate between breeding and feeding-sites. So far, three migration circuits have been studied.

There are the Caribbean green turtles, that head for Tortuguero in Costa Rica for egg-laying, the South Yemen population, and the mysterious Ascension Island contingent. In each case, it is likely that the evolution of the circuit bears some relationship to the direction of ocean currents.

At Tortuguero, for instance, both tagged turtles and drift bottles were released, and there is a remarkable similarity in their distribution.

It seems logical to assume that the currents are responsible, at least in part, for the movement of females from the breeding to the feeding-sites. After two years, about a third of the females return to the Tortuguero beach, the remainder arriving the following year. Similarly, females tagged and released from Mukalta, on the South Yemen coast, were found down-current on the 'horn of Africa'.

Carr and his colleagues released tagged turtles from the Ascension Island beaches and found all recoveries downstream along the Brazilian coast. In one experiment, of over 200 females tagged at Ascension, nine were caught by Brazilian fishermen, and five returned to the island. Could it be that the young hatchlings also follow the flow of the Equatorial Current to find their nursery sites? This is still a mystery. It is not until turtles are about ten years old, the age at which they are able to breed, that we can rejoin their story.

When mature they head off to the breeding beaches, but not all the Brazilian turtles go to Ascension. Some follow the northern fork of the south equatorial current and find beaches along the north-west coast of Brazil. Only the turtles that were hatched on Ascension return there. Explanations of how they find their way must be, for the present, pure speculation.

If the migrating adults were able to look over their shoulders they would see the receding coastline and start off in the right direction. At the other end, Ascension's 1500-metre-high mountain might guide them for the last 100 kilometres; that is, on a fine day with a calm sea. It is unlikely that these are suitable cues, for the turtle's problem is a precise one. It must swim across an area of ocean the shape of an isoceles triangle, with the sharp point at Ascension Island and a 200-kilometre base line, about 2000 kilometres away. Any guidance system must keep the turtles within the triangle. The problem looms even larger when you consider that individual turtles are far from bisymmetrical, sometimes push harder with one flipper than the other, and are often dragged to one side by barnacles growing on the carapace.

An appreciation of ocean currents could help navigation. The Equatorial Current always flows to the west. If a turtle swims against the prevailing current, it would head roughly in the right direction. Similarly, a suitable circular-current system would bring the animal, in a roundabout way, into approximately the right area. Turtles in the current that forks to the south along the Brazilian coast would eventually be swept around to the west with the West Wind Drift, northwards along the Atlantic coast of

Africa in the Beguela current, and back into the South Equatorial Current. This would mean time in very cold seas, however, and is therefore an unsuitable route for sea turtles. A counter-current at another depth is another possibility. The equatorial under-current flows eastwards at a depth of 100 metres along the line of the equator. This would also bring turtles into the right area. But, would it be precise enough for turtles to find Ascension? It seems unlikely.

Contained *in* an ocean current, though, might be a useful cue. By tasting the water, as it heads east, a turtle might be able to detect an olfactory gradient. An olfactory 'signature', drifting away from Ascension would gradually get weaker as it was diluted to the west. A turtle could follow the 'smell' back to the island, as it were, climbing an odour ladder.

Underwater sounds have been suggested as homing cues. Breakers crashing on to a beach would send considerable amounts of very low-frequency infra-sounds into the water. Ascension might have its own signature tune. Even more bizarre is the suggestion that turtles might be able to detect and appreciate the Coriolus Force. A creature at the equator is travelling faster in space than one further north or south. If turtles could appreciate the speed with which they were travel-ling related to celestial events then they could work out where they were on the earth's surface.

A more understandable navigational sense would involve the earth's magnetic field. Many animals have demonstrated the ability to detect magnetic fields (see Chapter 4), and it is tempting to seek a magnetic explanation in the case of the sea turtle. In several early experiments turtles have had bar magnets attached to their heads. At first they became disoriented, but adapted rapidly. If the magnets were allowed to spin, however, the turtles were unable to adapt. Geomagnetic cues look interesting.

Celestial cues are, perhaps, the most obvious navigational aids that turtles might use. Being air-breathers they must return to the surface in order to get a fresh lungful of air. Each time they put their heads out of the water they could take a compass bear-ing on the sun, the moon or the stars. In experiments with a moving artificial sun, Klaus Fischer, of Duke University, showed that turtles were able to locate objects accurately, relative to the position of the sun. As the Ascension Island turtles travel almost along the equator, a 'fix' every morning at sunrise would give the correct heading.

There is, however, yet another puzzle. Even if they can find their way, can they swim against the current? It has been estimated that a green turtle's maximum swimming speed is about 2 kilometres per hour. The South Equatorial Current flows westwards at about 1.85 kilometres per hour, so a turtle swimming flat out would only just be making any headway.

But, with this creature and its life so full of questions there still remains the most intriguing puzzle of them all. Why, with suitable breeding beaches on its doorstep, should these green turtles travel to Ascension Island?

The simplest answer, perhaps, is that the island was found quite by accident during an exploratory migration by a wandering individual. Long-distance migration is not unusual in the animal kingdom; witness birds, seals and fish. Green turtles always return to the beaches from whence they came and so, come hell or high water, they find their way back and the group habit is formed. The individual could have come from the West African coast, where there are many green turtle breeding and feeding-grounds. This explanation has the advantage of letting the turtles drift along effortlessly with the South Equatorial Current, and pitching up on Ascension, albeit on the wrong side. A further drift across the Atlantic and they reach Brazil.

There is, however, a more interesting story to be told, and that involves the theory of continental drift.

Ancestors of the modern green sea turtles were living over 100 million years ago in the seas between the North American sector of Laurasia, which was heading north, and the African section of Gondwanaland. They were herbivores, some growing to gigantic sizes, over 3 metres, and it is thought that their breeding areas were separate from their feeding-grounds, as they are today.

Small mammals were beginning to make their presence felt, in particular, those that had developed a taste for turtle eggs. These egg-predators forced the turtles to seek island sites for egg-laying.

A rift valley began to separate Africa and South America. It was eventually flooded to form a continuous Arctic-to-Antarctic Atlantic Ocean. The Mid-Atlantic ridge was formed, and magma extruding from the line of the ridge pushed out to either side, and slowly moved Africa to the east and South America to the west.

Along the ridge there were numerous undersea volcanoes. Some, like Tristan da Cunha and the Azores on today's ridge, reached the surface of the sea to become volcanic islands. After periods of marine erosion and deposition, the exposed volcanic beaches became ideal nesting-sites. Exploring turtles found them and returned regularly to lay their precious eggs. They swam the short distance to their feeding-grounds on the north-east coast of the recently separated continent of South America.

Sea-floor spreading continued, with Africa and South America slowly moving further apart; but more significantly, the oceanic volcanic islands were carried along with them, to each side of the spreading ridge. Eventually a small string of islands was formed from the ridge towards the Brazilian coast, each, in turn, proving attractive to female turtles seeking nest sites. All the volcanoes in the island chain became extinct, their volcanic throats cut from the magma chamber below the ridge. Islands furthest from the ridge were pounded by the sea, eventually disappearing below the waves to become underwater sea-mounts. The turtles, robbed of their nesting-sites, simply swam the extra few kilometres to the next island above water. Gradually, over millions of years, the gap grew to become the 2000-kilometre journey we see today.

Ascension Island was formed about 7 million years ago. Its predecessor, and previous host to the green turtles, is a sea-mount lying 1500 metres below the ocean surface, about 15 kilometres to the west.

An attractive feature of the theory is that in order to find each successive island all the turtles need do is head off towards the rising sun. One drawback is that the population would have had to be inbreeding for 70 or so million years, thereby accentuating any unique features, and there are no signs that the Ascension Island green turtles are any different from green turtles from other parts of the world. Another disadvantage is that any animal with a global distribution like the green sea turtle is not likely to be constrained by such a limiting navigation system, and confined to a particular migration circuit.

There is, however, evidence from the green turtle populations studied by Carr, that turtles on one migration circuit do not actually mix with others. They simply stick to their own routes.

There is no doubt that continental drift has had a profound effect on a number of animals, shaping migration patterns and living conditions, but the explanations that we can offer for the events that we see today can only be stabs in the dark. As Archie Carr once said, 'Animal migration research is merely an array of outrageous hypotheses. Depending on the state of your liver, you choose this one or that.'

# At the Bottom of the Sea

In 322 BC Alexander the Great was lowered beneath the surface of the Aegean Sea and was able to watch underwater life from the safety of a glass diving-bell. In 1977 John Corliss, John Edmond, and Jack Donnelly travelled in the US submersible, *Alvin*, to the bottom of the Pacific Ocean at the Galapagos Rift and saw a complete self-contained ecosystem never before seen by man.

Such is our knowledge of the oceans that in the 2000 years since Alexander was captivated by the wonders of the Mediterranean we can still enter that alien domain and be humbled by our ignorance of all it contains. William Beebe, in 1934, was one of the first to explore the mysteries of the deepest deeps in his spherical bathysphere. He was followed by August Piccard in the bathyscaphe, an underwater vessel that was to be the forerunner of the first oceanographic research submersibles.

In 1960 the submersible *Trieste* went down to a historic 10,915 metres in the Mariana Trench off Guam, and the age of deep-water exploration began in earnest. A boost to the study of the bottom of the sea came in 1966 with the inception of an 'International Decade of Ocean Exploration'. The 1970s brought us NORPAX – the North Pacific Experiment, MODE – the Mid-Oceans Dynamics Experiment, ISOS – the International Southern Oceans Study, GEOSECS – Geochemical Ocean Sections Study, FAMOUS – the French American Mid-Ocean Undersea Study and many others – CLIMAP, POLYMODE, CEPEX, SEAREX, PRIMA, MANOP, RISE, SEATAR, CENOP, CUEA, SES, and so on. The discovery of manganese nodules, rich in expensive minerals, just sitting on the sea-bed, ready to be scooped up, triggered a 'goldrush' of deep-sea exploration and gave rise to a decade of political manoeuvrings, known as 'The Law of the Sea Conference', aimed at carving up the sea-bed for the wealth that it could produce. Fortunately for science, there were many fascinating spin-offs, in particular, a greater understanding of the geophysical forces that have shaped the earth and the discovery of new life forms living at the bottom of the sea. For deep-sea explorers, Robert Ballard, of the Woods Hole Oceanographic Institution, Jean Francheteau, of the University of Paris, and Peter Lonsdale, of the Scripps Institution of Oceanography, perhaps the most extraordinary discovery was made on the Galapagos Rift expedition, early in 1977.

## Hot springs at the bottom of the sea

About 330 kilometres to the north-east of the Galapagos Islands is a rift valley on the ocean floor associated with a mid-oceanic spreading centre. Molten lava, oozing through a crack in the earth's crust from the mantle below, is forming the Cocos plate to the north and the Nazca plate to the south. The rift valley has been formed by the plates pulling apart along the boundary. A survey in 1972, by the Woods Hole Oceanographic Institution, revealed unusual temperature variations across the rift that suggested areas of hot water, much like the hot geysers on land.

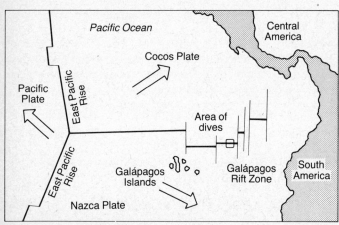

*Area of Galapagos Rift expedition.*

This was confirmed in another survey by Scripps in 1976, which found hot water and unusual chemistry suggestive of a hot-water discharge from the crust. The Scripps team left underwater transmitters on the sea bottom, and the following year, together with satellite navigational aids, Woods Hole research vessel *Knorr* was able to pinpoint this section of the rift for a closer investigation.

Under the direction of Robert Ballard, an unmanned sled (ANGUS), with cameras and electrical temperature sensors aboard, was put over the side and towed, back and forth, across the rift. Keeping the ship on course was not easy for a one-and-a-half knot current kept pushing it to the west. After six hours of watching and hoping, the instruments showed that the sled had passed over a hot-water anomaly. It lasted for about three minutes. It was the only 'contact' in a search lasting twelve hours and over 16 kilometres of sea-bed. The underwater camera had taken 3000 colour photographs.

The film was not removed for an agonising couple of hours so that the camera, which had been in freezing temperatures at the bottom, could warm up, and prevent condensation from destroying the pictures. The first part of the film showed barren ocean floor covered by pillow lava, followed by younger ropy flows of lava. Another section of pillow lava marked the boundary line of low volcanoes. Then suddenly, for thirteen frames, the ocean floor was covered with hundreds of clams and mussels in a patch of misty-blue water. On the fourteenth frame the shellfish once more were missing and the rest of the film showed barren lava. The thirteen frames coincided exactly with the temperature variation shown on the instruments the previous day.

With her work completed, and the area of warm water located, the *Knorr* moved off-station to be replaced by *Lulu*, support ship to the deep-sea manned submersible, *Alvin*. An underwater navigational system of transponders had been placed on the bottom of the rift which enabled *Alvin* to locate accurately the site as it dived, dropping at 30–35 metres per minute, virtually blind, to the bottom. It took an hour and a half to reach the ocean floor, about 2700 metres below the surface. It arrived just a couple of hundred metres away from the target area and moved along the bottom. First it crossed the pillow lava, and the crew inside could see the same barren underwater seascape that had featured in most of the photographs, but as it approached the crest of the rise, the researchers' attention was drawn to a couple of purple sea anemones. Then they noticed the water was shimmering, 'like air over a warm pavement'. As the submersible edged forward they saw the most incredible sight. Gushing from cracks in the lava was shimmering water that turned a dirty blue as minerals precipitated out and stained the rocks. All around were myriads of creatures, including giant clams up to 30 centimetres across that packed in dense clumps close to the vents. Here was an amazing community of animals living on an oasis of rock just 50 metres wide, on a hot-spring field in complete darkness. What, thought the researchers, could they be living on? The answer was quick to reveal itself. Samples taken back on board smelled of rotten eggs – hydrogen sulphide.

Cracks in the sea-bed allow cold water to percolate down into the newly forming crust. As it becomes heated its chemical nature changes and minerals from the surrounding rocks are leaked out. Sulphates combine with the hydrogen to form hydrogen sulphide, and the hot water rises to flow out of the ocean floor as hydrothermal vents. The sulphide becomes food for bacteria on which the other creatures in the community can feed, thus a food chain is formed in association with the vents, and nowhere else on the rift valley floor. Deep-sea communities usually depend on detritus from the surface waters sinking to the ocean depths but the hydrothermal vent ecosystem is unique, for unlike other communities on earth, it is independent of the energy provided by the sun. The energy comes directly from the centre of the earth.

## Clambake, Dandelion Patch and the Garden of Eden

During the 1977 expedition several hydrothermal vents were found. Unfortunately, no biologists were aboard to identify the life forms present, but it quickly became apparent that no two vents were alike. They gained, however, a colourful set of nicknames.

'Clambake I' was packed with giant white clams and brown mussels. They were packed so tightly that they channelled the water flow, like living conduits. Crawling over and around them were white crabs, and floating above was an occasional purple octopus, a sole predator. 'Clambake II' was dead. Scattered across the lava flows were dead clam and mussel shells, slowly disintegrating in water devoid of lime. The hot water flow had, for some reason, shut off. 'Dandelion Patch' was the third site, with an abundance of creatures that looked like dandelion seed heads attached to the sea floor by an intricate webbing of fine fibres. The fourth site's nickname of 'Oyster Bed' showed up the absence of a marine biologist for subsequent research revealed that not one oyster could be found there! The fifth site was dubbed the 'Garden of Eden' on account of the diversity of life forms. They were present in a series of concentric rings, each ring dominated by a particular species. White crabs and 'dandelions' were found in the outer ring, followed by a circle of spider-like tube-worms attached to the rock surface. Closest to the mouth of the vent were limpets, pink fish and enormous tube-worms with red tops.

In January and February 1979, a team of biologists joined the geologists and chemists on the next Galapagos expedition. Their aim was to establish the distribution and structure of the life forms present around the vents, and examine the way that these creatures have adapted to their unusual habitat.

The water from the active hydrothermal vents has been described as 'milky-blue', indicating to biologists that oxidation of the hydrogen sulphide by the vent bacteria could provide the energy required to fix carbon dioxide into organic matter. This parallels the way that surface organisms use sunlight as the energy source in photosynthesis. Bacterial counts of the vent water have indicated high levels of organisms present, and there are many different types. Those directly in the vents showed uniformity of structure, but were commonly found in clumps. There were also free-living spirochaetes, and on the surfaces of the rocks and shellfish the researchers found a network of filamentous, stalked bacteria (prosthecate bacteria). It is thought that the greatest production of bacteria takes place, not on the sea floor, but in growth chambers further down inside the vents.

Some of the less obvious organisms to be found at the hydrothermal vents live in the sediments. Microscopic protozoans, rarely seen before, are very common. Of special interest is a flower-like xenophyophorian. This belongs to the largest group of protozoans, that possess rigid flake-like bodies from which pseudopodia, up to 12 centimetres long, protrude.

The spider-like tube-worms, seen on the geophysical expedition, turned out to be enteropneusts – acorn-worms. These are a group of marine worm-like creatures, in the phylum Hemichordata, that were once thought to be related to primitive chordate animals, for they have a proboscis strengthened by a forward running tube that was mistaken for a notochord. Shallow water species are usually found in mud, and are filter feeders. The newly found deep-sea relatives were dubbed 'spaghetti' and have been hauled to the surface where they are meriting further study.

'Dandelions' were found to fragment when disturbed and only one intact specimen was brought to the surface. It was recognised as a siphonophore, very similar to those discovered on the *Challenger* voyage of 1872–6. Siphonophores are hydrozoan coelenterates (related to the Portuguese man-of-war) in that they consist of colonies of miniature sea anemone-like

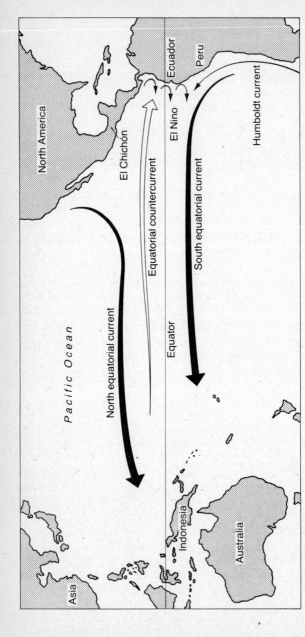

*Trade winds blow from east to west. If they weaken, the cold waters of the Humboldt current are submerged and severe storms occur in South America.*

hydroids, each of which is specialised for a digestive, stinging or reproductive function, to the benefit of the entire animal. The 'dandelion' siphonophores are yellow balls of hydroids, surrounded by long, thin hair-like filaments that raise the creature off the sea bottom.

Near the 'Garden of Eden' site two more vent areas were identified: Mussel Bed, and Rose Garden, so-named on account of the red tube-worms living there.

The red vestimentiferan worms *Riftia pachyptila* live in tough, flexible tubes, up to 3 metres in length. Extending from one end is a bright red plume. The distinct colour is derived from the oxygenated haemoglobin in the blood. They have no gut. Around the base of the large specimens were found clusters of juvenile worms in tubes only 15 centimetres long. They were thought, at first, to be pogonophorans, but have now been assigned a group of their own.

Crustaceans were represented by shrimp-like leptostracans, brachyuran crabs and squat lobsters. The shrimp is unusual in that it has comb-like structures on the stalks where its eyes should be, a configuration never seen before. It is thought that the combs are used to scrape food organisms from the rock surface. The squat lobsters (Galatheidae), particularly females with large egg batches, were sitting on the tops of the pillow lavas and were seen to be very active. The white brachyuran or true crabs were found close to the vents. Laboratory studies revealed that they have a slower metabolic rate than their shallow water cousins, but they could survive at temperatures greater than 22°C at the bottom pressure.

Giant mussels and clams, in dense clusters, surrounded the vents. The clams, *Galyptogena magnifica*, were up to 26 centimetres long. They have red blood, unlike other bivalves, and smell like meat. Laboratory tests showed the largest to be about ten years old. Some of the mussels were found with pearls. Others played host to polychaete worms.

Members of the 1979 expedition, like their predecessors, noticed that the creatures were grouped into zones at certain distances from the vent. Furthest away, on isolated pillow lava formations, was the occasional sea cucumber, sea anemone or coral. Nearer the vent, but at the edge of the warm water area, were the crabs, the 'spaghetti' enteroneusts, and the 'dandelions'. In a 2°C temperature zone around the vent the most creatures were found, with clam and mussel beds, fan-worms and sea anemones. Close to the vent, the tops of the rocks are inhabited by fan-worms and squat lobsters. Next to the vents were the vestimentiferan worms, and on the lining of the vent walls and sides of the worm tubes were light-coloured limpets. They were joined in the vents by pink, elongated brotulid fish, a new species of copepod (Spinocalanidae), and *Onesimus* amphipods.

At the bottom of the food chain of the hydrothermal vent community are the sulphur bacteria. Clams, mussels and other filter feeders clearly sieve them from the warm waters, but it was not obvious how the gutless tube-worms tapped into the system. Dissolved organic molecules could be absorbed from the sea water via the red tentacles, but this would provide insufficient nutrients for the animal to keep going; they are, after all, nearly 2 metres long and 40 centimetres in diameter. Dissection of the worms has revealed a mass of cells, with a good blood supply, near the gonads in the trunk region of the body. The tissue has been found to contain sulphur crystals, and scientists at Scripps at first speculated on the worms metabolising sulphur and fixing carbon just as the vent bacteria are doing. Closer inspection, though, revealed symbiotic bacteria present in the tissue. The tube-worms' diet, it seems, is supplemented by substances manufactured by the bacteria.

## The chimneys of hell at 21° north

In 1979, *Alvin* and mothership *Lulu* took part in the Rivera Submersible Experiments Programme (RISE). The action had moved further north, in fact, to latitude 21° north, where the Pacific and Rivera plates are separating at the rate of 6 centimetres a year. The boundary zone is known as the East Pacific Rise. The researchers were interested in the area of the crest, the place at which new crust is created and where the beginnings of crustal movements can be studied.

Once again ANGUS was used to survey the area, which had already been looked over by the French CYAMEX expedition with their submersible *Cyana* in 1978, and the usual sea-floor transponders were deployed to guide *Alvin*. What they discovered has led to some of the most exciting and significant recent developments in oceanography. There, on the plate boundary crest, the submersible teams found enormous black chimneys, spewing out, at 350°C, inky-coloured water that contained iron, copper, nickel and zinc. They were nicknamed the 'black smokers', the black colour coming from an iron sulphide precipitate. They towered above the submersibles for several metres, and had numerous side vents forming complex structures. At the very high pressure in the deep sea, hot water at over 300°C does not turn to steam as it would in terrestrial geysers, but remains liquid. So, instead of periodic and explosive activity, like that seen in Yellowstone, these hot submarine springs gush water continuously, depositing valuable minerals on the ocean floor.

Three types of vents were identified by the RISE team – hot-water black smokers, white chimneys, and the Galapagos-type warm-water vents. A similar fauna to that seen at Galapagos was found around the warm-water vents, with the exception of anemones and giant mussels. The black smokers appear to have very little associated life, but the hot-water white chimneys were found to have distinctive faunas.

The water leaving white chimneys appeared milky-white and was at temperatures between 30 and 330°C. The chimneys were covered with criss-cross clumps of worm tubes, some in the shape of cylinders and others like ragged 'snowballs'. The white snowballs capped hot-water vents with water at 330°C, and consisted of a complex sponge-like tube of pink polychaete worms that were seen to leave their tubes completely, forage in the hot water, and then return to safety when approached by a crab or fish. Around the vents were squat lobsters, crabs and eel-like fish. On one dive a 'new-to-science', primitive, short-stalked, scalpellid barnacle was found. What, though, do these hot-water creatures depend on for food? Could there be bacteria living in the vents?

## Some like it hot

The temperatures and pressures at deep-sea hot hydrothermal vents are such that life would not be expected to survive. The pressure is about 250 atmospheres and the temperature of the vent water goes up to 350° Centigrade, yet bacteria grow here in profusion. Most plants and animals succumb at 40°C, and most bacteria are killed between 70 and 100°C. Bacterial spores are in normal circumstances thought to be killed by sterilisation at 120°C. Sulphur bacteria from hot springs have been found to live in waters at 105°C, but these have until now been the record breakers. The discovery that bacteria could live in waters at temperatures of 250°C or more has prompted excited scientists to reassess the origins of life on earth and speculate on life elsewhere on and *in* the planet, and also in other parts of the universe.

The hot-vent bacteria are primitive archaebacteria, a separate evolutionary line from the 'true' bacteria. They probably evolved at an early stage in the earth's history, and their high-temperature resistance might indicate a much earlier date for the origins of life than had been thought previously. To endure the prevailing conditions, the microbes must have proteins and enzymes that are stable at such temperatures, a factor that has led several biochemists to suggest a commercial interest from washing-powder manufacturers and others using enzyme systems at high temperatures. It has also been shown that large quantities of hydrogen gas and methane are produced as products of metabolism. Might this form the basis of a potentially useful and lucrative industry for the manufacture of natural gas?

John Baross, of Oregon State University, and Jody Deming, of Johns Hopkins University, have cultured the vent bacteria in the laboratory. Under high pressures the temperature of water can be raised considerably without it boiling. This the researchers achieved with a pressure vessel containing water, minerals and vent bacteria. They found that the bacteria thrived in water at 250°C (the temperature limit for the apparatus being used) – the higher the temperature, the better the bacteria reproduced.

Research is currently aimed at building a vessel that could be taken to higher temperatures and pressures in order to establish the upper limit.

Probes placed in the hydrothermal vents where the samples were taken recorded temperatures of 308°C. Could it be that further down the vent there are organisms living at still higher temperatures – a whole new flora as yet unknown to man? Does this also mean that life could be represented on planets in the solar system that were hitherto thought to be completely hostile – for example, on Venus, despite the enormous surface pressures and temperatures? And finally, should we rethink the start of life on our own planet, not as a one-off event many millions of years ago, but as a continuous process still going on today? The findings at deep-sea hydrothermal vents will certainly give more respectability to those searching for life elsewhere in the universe.

## Temples and pagodas
As if to underline our ignorance of the ocean depths, yet another startling discovery was made when Peter Lonsdale examined the sea floor of the Guaymas basin in the Gulf of California. Here the East Pacific Rise marks the rift that is separating the Baja

peninsula from the mainland. Instead of pillow lava formation, the magma exudes through thick, coarse-grained sediments and silts. Hydrothermal activity is confined to the insides of enormous mounds of sediment, which Lonsdale found along the axis of the spreading centre. The ascending magma forms sills and dykes, and the deposition of ores takes place within the hydrothermal network in the mounds. One major difference from the other mid-ocean hydrothermal systems is the abundance of biological activity in the surrounding waters. This means that a lot of planktonic debris falls on to the ocean floor, making the silt rich in carbon. Sediment cores taken by the Guaymas basin expedition smelled of diesel oil, and the water samplers of *Alvin* were clogged by globules of wax. It appears that the complex organic molecules are broken down by the heat of the hydrothermal fields into hydrocarbons, which are, in turn, fed on by bacteria. The Guaymas basin is characterised by mats of bacteria that compete with worms, crabs, and clams for space around the vents.

The vents themselves are amazing structures in the shape of Japanese pagodas. They have been found along the ridges of the 100-metre-long mounds. The water is an uncomfortable 315°C, but nevertheless, tube-worms and bacteria mats are living close to the hot water. Further away, black coral grows in long 'hedge-rows' and large red crabs joust with large white octpuses. Two strange fish were trapped in the hatch area of *Alvin* and brought to the surface. They are, as yet, unidentified, but have been dubbed the '21° north vent fish'. Little white dots on the rocks, seen in the underwater photographs, turned out to be a new species of marine snail.

With all these recent remarkable discoveries, attention is being focused on activity at other mid-ocean spreading centres. The first to be found were the Red Sea Brines, hot areas on the floor of the Red Sea where mineral salts have been precipitated as a result of hydrothermal activity within the deposits. The process had been similar to that in the Guaymas basin except that salt ponds, concentrated when the Red Sea dried up during the Miocene period, were substituted for carbon-rich sediments. At the Marianas spreading centre in the western Pacific another hydrothermal vent system is associated with mounds of volcanic deposits. And, along the Mid-Atlantic Ridge, a slow-moving centre, there is some evidence of similar hydrothermal activity. Large clams were seen on the crest of the Reykjanes Ridge during a dive of the US Navy nuclear-powered submersible

*NR-1*, and hydrothermal activity is thought to have been detected at 27° north.

Having been flooded with this wealth of discovery, the marine biologists are now taking stock of the available data and attempting to answer fundamental questions – how do these vent systems become colonised? The vents are, essentially, oases on the sterile basaltic ocean bottom. Is there a traffic between vent system and, if so, are the biological communities that have been found in the few hydrothermal fields explored to date, universal in their distribution?

# A Change in the Weather

The climate in various parts of the world has not always been the same as it is today. Movements of the continents, the rise and fall of sea-levels, and changes in atmospheric circulation have meant that cold places have become hot, hot places cold, dry countries wet and wet ones dry. The Sahara, for example, has been variously a shallow sea, a swamp and the desert we see today. Not that long ago tropical plants and animals lived along the south coast of Britain. Their fossils can be found in the rocks of ancient cave-sites like those of the Gower peninsula and the Mendips. Today the south coast has a temperate climate. Tomorrow, who knows?

Researchers, however, are trying to find out, and the sciences of climatology and meteorology have become important disciplines in the understanding of how the physical changes on our planet affect the survival of life as we know it. Almost daily, reports come in that suggest the earth is warming up at an alarming rate. An increase in global carbon dioxide ($CO_2$) levels caused by the burning of fossil fuels like coal and oil, and the drastic reduction in forests around the world (trees use up carbon dioxide during photosynthesis in daylight hours) may give rise to a phenomenon known as the 'greenhouse effect'. Even termites have been held responsible. One researcher proposed that they produce so much methane while munching their way through their cellulose foods, that they contribute substantially to the $CO_2$ content of the atmosphere. The blanket of $CO_2$ effectively acts like the glass of a greenhouse, allowing light and heat to pass through but trapping the infra-red radiation inside. The consequences could be devastating. The polar ice-caps would melt, raising the level of the oceans considerably. The wheat belts of North America would become deserts. Coastal areas, where many countries concentrate their industrial complexes, would be under many metres of water. Studies of the Antarctic ice by the British Antarctic Survey have shown that there are already detectable changes that could be the precursors of a global rise in temperature.

Climate might also be influenced by factors outside the planet – from space. Sun spots on the solar disc are often followed by magnetic storms on earth, for example. But perhaps the most frightening prospect is being hit by some gigantic extra-terrestrial body, say a comet or a meteorite. Just recently two comets flew dangerously close to our vulnerable planet. Iras-Araki-Alcock came to within 5 million kilometres on 23 January 1982, and Sugano-Saigusa-Fujikawa to about 6 million on 10 April 1982, both near-misses on the astronomical scale. If one had hit the planet it is likely that masses of rock, dust and steam would have been flung into the atmosphere, blocking out the light from the sun, and thereby cutting off that vital source of energy for life on earth. Could such an event have been responsible for the demise of the dinosaurs? There is good evidence to suggest that this might have been the case.

## The time of great dying

At Gubbio, in Italy, the road slices through layers of pink and white limestone that hold the key to the dinosaur mystery. At one road-cutting in the Bottaccione Gorge, the boundary between two great geological ages can be found. It is represented by a thin layer of brown clay. Below the line the sediments were deposited in a deep-sea in the Cretaceous period, the period that ended about 65 million years ago. Above the line are the red limestones that were laid down at the beginning of the Tertiary period. The line also marks the time that the dinosaurs ended their reign on earth, and an enormous number of species of both plants and animals became extinct.

Microscopic examination of the Cretaceous sediments shows that the sea must have been crowded with a microscopic single-celled foraminifera, with minute calcareous shells that became fossilised in the rock, and called *Globotruncana*. In the clay layer it disappears altogether, and in the Tertiary rocks above is found a close relative, *Globigerina*, that seems to have made a come-back. Walter Alvarez, a geologist from the University of California at Berkeley has been studying these rocks. He was trying to determine the ages of the rocks at Gubbio by searching for known reversals of the earth's magnetic field that show up in the various layers. In a conversation with his father, the Nobel physicist Luis Alvarez, of the Lawrence Berkeley Laboratory at Berkeley, Alvarez Jnr began to intrigue his father with the fossil differences above and below the boundary clay layer and, together with Helen Michel and Frank Asaro, they began a chemical investigation. The most significant result was the discovery of large amounts of the rare metal iridium in the clay.

Iridium is not very abundant on the earth itself but is common in meteorites. If an enormous asteroid had hit the earth 65 million years ago, argued Alvarez Snr, then dust from the impact would be rich in iridium. The cloud, having first encircled the earth in the stratosphere, would slowly be deposited all around the globe, and would be represented today by the clay layer. The search started for other exposures of rocks from the Cretaceous-Tertiary boundary. These were duly found in Denmark, New Zealand and North America. In each case the boundary sediments show greatly increased iridium levels. In Italy the level is thirty times greater than would be expected, in Denmark 160 times, and in New Zealand twenty times. Whatever had caused the increased levels had certainly affected the whole of the planet. Alvarez Snr first proposed an earth-crossing asteroid as the culprit. He reasoned that about sixty times the object's mass would be thrown into the atmosphere as pulverised rock, and that much of the dust would circle the earth for several years. The dust would blot out the sun, and the darkness would deprive plants of the energy necessary for photosynthesis. This would affect mainly the microscopic phytoplankton in the oceans, which in turn would upset the feeding of the zooplankton. With the base of the food chain disrupted, other creatures in the sea would be affected.

The fossil record appears to show just what might be expected. The microscopic floating plants and animals reached near-extinction. Higher up the chain the belemnites and ammonites, cephalopods that had been on the earth for over 300 million years, disappeared altogether. Marine reptiles, such as the fish-like ichthyosaurs and the long-necked plesiosaurs which grew to 50 metres, died off completely (except, maybe, the one in Loch Ness, so some would have us believe).

On land the plants ceased to produce new growth and many rode out the dark period as seeds, spores, or root stock. The giant herbivore reptiles, such as the sauropods, *Diplodocus* and *Brachiosaurus*, had nothing to eat, and with their demise also went the giant carnivores, such as the 15-metre-high *Tyrannosaurus*. No terrestrial animal larger than 25 kilograms is thought to have survived. The ancestors of the mammals *did* pull through, as did the first birds. The enormous soaring pterosaurs fell out of the skies. Snakes made it, as did the crocodiles and the small lizards. When the going gets tough a small creature can hide under boulders or in cracks and crevices, and maybe even hibernate during the worst periods.

Alvarez's story seemed plausible, but the scientific community was sceptical. Debate was heated; after all, nearly every scientist you meet has his own view of these mass extinctions. Where did the extra-terrestrial object come from, they asked, and where might it have landed?

Periodically the earth does collide with large objects in space. There are several craters that can still be recognised, even after erosion of their main features, but they are the wrong age. There are the remains of a large crater at Manicouagan, near Quebec, 70 kilometres across and dated at 210 before the present, and another two in the Soviet Union dated 38 million years and 183 million. We cannot, however, see evidence of those bodies that might have hit the ocean basins as they are quickly buried by ocean sediments. Might there be a link between known collisions and mass extinctions? Some researchers believe there are.

In the 570 million years of the earth's history for which we have ample fossil remains to make an assessment of plant and animal populations, there have been at least seven great extinctions, and of those, five are possible contenders for an extra-terrestrial impact hypothesis. They were: in the late Ordovician, which ended about 446 million years ago; at the Frasnian-Fammennian border of the Mid-Upper Devonian about 336 million years ago; at the Permian-Triassic border about 247 million years ago; in the late Triassic about 220 million years ago; and at the Cretaceous-Tertiary border about 65 million years ago. The other two extinctions were earlier, at the end of the Cambrian and in the early Ordovician.

To take just one event, the Frasnian-Fammennian border, the fossil record shows a time of great change, when sudden anatomical adaptations are seen and a marked reduction in numbers of certain animal groups. In the Frasnian period there was an explosion of species of corals. Trilobites, crinoids, and brachiopods lived alongside them in the sea. Stromatoporoids were abundant. These are thought to have been sponges that were on the earth for 75 million years. But, in the Fammennian period only solitary corals are found, the ammonites changed drastically, one genus of trilobites remained, and the stromatoporoids all but disappeared. Could it have been that worldwide climatic changes triggered by dust in the atmosphere from a cosmic collision caused the demise of these creatures as well?

Closer examination of the fossil record shows that these major events are only the most obvious to spot. Between them appear many minor events. Indeed, studies of the microfossils in ocean sediments reveal a periodicity of about 30 million years, give or take a few million. In 1977 A. G. Fischer, of Princeton University, suggested a pattern of extinctions every 32 million years, but few listened to him. Then, in October 1983 David Raup and John Sepkoski, of the University of Chicago, announced some exciting results from their study of marine fossils. They suggested that the 247, 220, and 65-million-year-old extinctions had each resulted in the disappearance of 95 per cent of the species then on earth. On seven other occasions only 20 to 50 per cent were lost, and they were dated at 194, 163, 144, 125, 91, 38, and 11 million years ago. This revealed a periodicity of about 26 to 28 million years. What could account for this regular happening? Enter the astrophysicists.

Two research groups working independently, one at Berkeley, and the other from the University of South-west Louisiana, published a plausible explanation. The sun, they said, has a companion star. They disagreed on size, shape and brightness but nevertheless came up with the same basic hypothesis. One group went as far as giving it a name – Nemesis. Nemesis and our sun are a binary star system. With elliptical orbits, they whizz around each other sometimes close together, at other times far apart. The companion closes in on our sun, so the theory goes, every 26 million years or so. As Nemesis enters the Oort comet cloud, about half a million light years away, all hell breaks loose, and comets upset by the gravitational influence of the companion star begin to fly in all directions, some heading towards earth. The odd one slams into the planet kicking up a heap of dust, the sun is excluded, plants cannot photosynthesise, and extinctions are the order of the day. Darkness, the researchers suggest, may last for a million years, and on present calculations the next event is about 15 million years away. Earth, of course, is not the only planet in our solar system to receive these visitors. There is speculation that the ring system around some of the giant planets is a result of an invasion of comets. There was, in fact, a suggestion some years ago that the earth itself had a ring system which accounted for the darkness on the planet, rather than a dust cloud in the atmosphere. The companion star hypothesis has made a good story, and indeed astronomers are now looking for a faint glow in the heavens that might give away its position, but it is not the only explanation.

At the Goddard Institute for Space Studies in New York another team explains away the darkness. Periodically the earth and the rest of the solar system pass through the arms of our spiral galaxy, the Milky Way. The sun influences comets as it passes through dense interstellar dust clouds, which rain down on the planets. Alternatively, the clouds might deposit excesses of chemicals like hydrogen in the upper atmosphere, causing worldwide pollution.

At present, it is not clear which hypothesis is more acceptable, and some scientists dismiss the whole thing as coincidence. Might there be evidence from earth? Walter Alvarez thinks there is. He suggests that evidence of impacts from extra-terrestrial bodies can be found in the craters that pock-mark the surface of our planet. Interestingly the craters, when dated, fall into the same cycle of 28 million years as the mass extinctions.

Another line of study looks at the implications that periodic extinctions might have for evolution. Clearly, extra-terrestrial events can change the composition of life on earth dramatically. Newly evolving species that survive the cataclysm get a boost. Without the great extinctions life may not have evolved in the way that it has. Trilobites, say, may have been ruling the earth today. It is fun to speculate. Palaeontologist Dale Russell did just that with the dinosaurs and came up with a reptilian humanoid with a big brain, which walked upright, as the creature to fill the ecological niche at present occupied by man. He even identified a likely ancestor in the fossil record – the 3-metre high *Stenonychosaurus inequalus*, that possessed a brain-to-body weight ratio similar to that of man. Nemesis, perhaps, saved man from appearing on earth as a refugee from an episode of *Dr Who*.

If, as seems likely, an extra-terrestrial impact gave rise to the dust clouds that blocked out the sun, is there any evidence that such clouds curtail plant growth? For an answer we have to examine the behaviour of volcanoes. Many times in the earth's history gigantic volcanic eruptions have been responsible for ejecting huge quantities of dust into the atmosphere. Krakatoa was one of the biggest in recent years, when 7.5 cubic kilometres of debris were thrown 30 kilometres into the air. The cloud encircled the globe. But, for evidence of the disturbance of photosynthesis we have to look back a little further, about 1500 years ago to a period between AD 536 and 537 when 'the densest and most persistent dry fog on record was observed in Europe and the Middle East'.

Space scientist R. B. Stothers has been digging into the agricultural records of the past and he suggests that the dry volcanic fog in AD 536 had a greater effect on climate and growth than any other volcanic cloud in the past 3000 years. Procopius, a Byzantine historian living in Rome, noted that the sun and the moon seemed to be in eclipse for the entire year. Lydus, in Constantinople, also recorded a dimming of the sun's rays 'so that the fruits were killed at an unseasonable time'. That 'the fruits did not ripen and the wine tasted like sour grapes' was revealed from sources in Mesopotamia. The volcano responsible for this abomination of a vintage is likely to have been Raboul, on the island of New Britain, off New Guinea. It erupted at about the right time, and the distribution of its debris around the world was confirmed from analysis of the deep snow and ice layers in the permanent Greenland ice-cap. These are similar to tree rings in that they date climatic events of the past. There is a problem, however, in blaming the Raboul volcano for the long period of restricted sunlight that the historians record. Volcanic dust settles very quickly – in a matter of weeks – so how could the prolonged cold spell be accounted for? The answer came quite recently, and it also went some way to explain the likely mechanism for the climatic conditions that may have given rise to the mass extinctions of the past.

In the spring of 1982 the Mexican volcano El Chichon blew its top. The eruption ejected enormous amounts of ash and volcanic gases high into the stratosphere, about 25 kilometres above the surface of the earth. The bang was relatively modest, as eruptions go, and the remoteness of the volcano in Mexico's southernmost state, Chiapas, meant that it escaped the attention of the world's press. The explosions were on a scale with those of Mount St Helens in May 1982, but differed in that, after the ash and dust had settled out, a fine mist of sulphuric acid droplets was left floating in the stratosphere. The cloud gradually spread to the west until it girdled the earth. In one year it had enveloped the Northern Hemisphere and the best part of the south. The droplets absorbed (and are still absorbing as I write, for it will take several years for the cloud to disperse) some of the energy reaching the earth from the sun, and this has been responsible for a drop in the overall average temperature on the surface of the planet. The cooling has probably affected the temperature distribution in the atmosphere and altered general circulation patterns. It has been suggested that the eruption of El Chichon contributed to the devastating changes that took place in atmospheric and ocean circulation in the equatorial Pacific – a phenomenon known as El Nino, the Christ Child.

## El Nino

El Nino is not an unusual event in itself, for it occurs every four to thirty years and is known to meteorologists as the 'southern oscillation'. In October or November the ocean currents that bathe the west coast of South America begin to change. The south-east trade winds die down, and the warm waters of the western Pacific Ocean surge around to the east, pushing down the cold waters of the Humboldt Current that normally flow northwards along the coast from the Antarctic. It usually results in unsettled weather and severe storms in South America and a failure of South America's west coast anchovy fisheries. Of the last nine El Ninos since 1950, only two have been abnormal – the one in 1982 that started in May instead of October, and another in 1963 that interestingly followed the eruption of Mount Agung, an event that similarly sent a fine sulphurous mist into the stratosphere.

Under normal circumstances air along the equator is heated. It rises, spreads to north and south, cools and sinks, only to sweep back into the tropical belt again as the Trade Winds. When the air in the upper parts of the atmosphere is warmed by the build-up of heat in volcanic mist ejected into the stratosphere, the rise of hot air is reduced and the Trade Winds begin to fail. In the case of this recent event, however, it is likely that the first signs of the coming disaster were noticed *before* the El Chichon eruption. The volcano only made matters worse. When the atmospheric circulation is running normally, Indonesia and North Australia constitute a low-pressure area, with warm air rising, cooling and spreading to areas of high pressure at places like Tahiti and Easter Island. Early in 1982 the reverse began to happen. Abnormally low atmospheric pressures were recorded at Easter Island in the south-east sector of the Pacific Ocean. At Darwin, in the Northern Territory of Australia, the pressure was high. Warm water that is actually blown and built up in the western side of the Pacific by the Trade Winds began to flow to the east as the winds slackened. Patches of warm water were reported at several places across the equatorial Pacific. The sea-level at Guadalcanal in the western Pacific dropped by 15 centimetres, while it rose by 15–25 centimetres around Fanning and Christmas islands in the central Pacific. A surge of warm water headed for the Galapagos Islands and the South American continent. The warm, southward-flowing Peru Coastal Under-current more than doubled its speed. Sea temperatures rose dramatically – by 5°C at the Galapagos Islands.

The atmospheric pressure systems continued to reverse until the highest atmospheric pressure this century was recorded at Darwin, and the lowest pressure for fifty years was monitored in Tahiti. This was to be no ordinary El Nino.

The impairment of rising hot air over Indonesia resulted in a severe drought over much of Australia. Forest fires raged through the south, destroying forests, devastating homes, and killing seventy-five people. Red dust storms, thousands of metres high and tens of thousands of square kilometres in extent, smothered cities. Widespread drought resulted in the destruction of millions of head of livestock. Damage was estimated to be in the order of 2500 million US dollars. In the Philippines crops failed and more than 350 islanders died of starvation. Damage was estimated to be in the order of 750 million dollars. An enormously powerful hurricane hit Hawaii, and several furious tropical cyclones sliced through French Polynesia leaving at least 25,000 Tahitians homeless. In Ecuador and northern Peru landslides after abnormally high rains left 600 people dead. A reservoir burst its dam. Continuous rains meant an accumulation of mosquito-infested water in numerous pools and lakes. Diseases were rife. On the west coast of the USA storms eroded coastlines, damaging property and roads because of extremely high tides, on-shore swells and giant waves. Damage was estimated at 1100 million dollars. More than 10,000 families lost their homes.

Despite the devastation and suffering, some good may have come out of the 1982 event, for it was the most studied El Nino in history. A quarter of the globe became a natural laboratory in which not only the physical oceanic and atmospheric systems were studied but also the resilience of plants and animals. Wild-life took quite a pounding too. Individual creatures tended not to consider the continuation of the family line but the durability of the individual. Reproduction was curtailed and survival dominated.

The Humboldt Current normally moves ice-cold water north-wards along the west coast of South America to the equator. The Galapagos Islands are an enigma as far as islands go for they have tropical lizards living alongside polar penguins and seals. Upwellings of nutrient-rich water provide raw materials on which the plankton flourishes, subsequently to be eaten by the fish, which are in turn prey for millions of sea-birds. When the Humboldt was suppressed the nutrients did not reach the plankton and it thinned considerably, as did the fish. With very little food the sea-birds came under threat.

Unfortunately, the main effects of El Nino came at nesting time. All along the west coast of the Americas from Alaska to Chile sea-birds vacated their nests and flew far out to sea where the influence of the surge of warm water was less strong. On Anacapa Island, off southern California, brown pelican chicks, almost ready for fledging, were left to die. Fur seal mothers on Galapagos abandoned their pups. Nature has a cruel way of conserving resources.

On Christmas Island the entire population of 17 million sea-birds, mostly terns, frigate birds and wedge-tailed shearwaters, and including the world's largest colony of 14 million sooty terns, upped and went. Many died in their fruitless search for food in the warm, barren sea, and hundreds of chicks still in the nests died from starvation. At the Farallon Islands, off the coast near San Francisco, ornithologists noticed that the spring upwellings, normally marked by blooms of phytoplankton, were absent. Euphausiid shrimps or krill made no appearance. They prefer water temperatures of between 9 and 11°C, and the ocean temperature had risen to 13°. The rock fish that prey upon the shrimps failed to turn up. The sea-birds, mainly auklets and murres, had no food. Of the 44,000 murres that attempted to breed only 500 actually fledged chicks. Very few of the 20,000 Brandt's cormorants bothered to turn up at all.

At Ano Nuevo the elephant-seal population took a heavy toll as pups were washed into the surf. Extraordinary high tides brought in storms that pounded the breeding beaches. Along the Californian coast species from warmer waters suddenly appeared. Marlin swam into Santa Barbara. Red crabs and sea-horses from Mexico turned up at San Francisco. West Coast religious freaks predicted Armageddon.

Under the sea, corals were found to be dead or dying. Thousands of square kilometres of coral reefs were located in the eastern Pacific, around French Polynesia, off the Philippines and Indonesia. Along the east coast of Panama, in the Atlantic, reefs were also dying.

The rare Galapagos marine iguanas came near to extinction. Their food, seaweeds such as *Ulva, Spermothamnium, Centroceras* and *Gelidium*, disappeared from the rocky coasts as a result of changes in salinity and water temperature. The normal algae were replaced by other species that the iguanas seemed unable to digest. The higher sea-levels associated with the surge, 22 centimetres higher than usual at Galapagos, also prevented the lizards from reaching their normal grazing places on the rocks. On some of the islands it was estimated that half the iguanas had died and the rest were dangerously underweight. The drop in salinity around the islands was due to the unusually heavy rains that had hit South America. The islands, normally dry and dusty, suddenly burst into a phase of luscious growth. Land birds, like the finches, had large clutches of eggs and some had up to five clutches in the season. Fledglings of the current season also nested and had eggs. Scientists travelling around the islands had to use machetes to get through the undergrowth on clifftops. The giant land tortoises had a superabundance of food. On Tower Island the researchers reported more rain falling in two weeks than had fallen in the previous six years. Butterflies appeared in profusion. The mosquito and horsefly populations went up, to the annoyance of all. Fire ants, it was found, began to take over new territories ten times faster than usual.

As I write, El Nino is in decline, and biologists are beginning to see how natural populations can recover from such a cataclysmic event. The Indian monsoon was normal, Australia's drought has broken and it has stopped raining in South America. The sea surface temperature in the middle of the Pacific has dropped by 4°C, and the Trade Winds are blowing as the major atmospheric pressure centres get back to normal. The birds are returning to Christmas Island, and the plankton blooms in the upwellings, that keep the ecosystem going, are richer than ever.

Those creatures that were able to change their diet or move long distances seem to have survived unscathed. Jackass penguins, for example, switched to squid and shrimps instead of their usual anchovies. But not all is well. Along the west coast of North America the plankton count has been down 90 per cent. Fish, like the hake and the mackerel, did not spawn when they should. The giant kelp beds that characterised the Oregon and Californian coasts and in which the rare sea otter lives, have been considerably reduced. Some beds have disappeared altogether.

In January 1985 scientists will be launching TOGA, a ten-year programme in which satellites, research vessels, and a wide-spread deployment of monitoring instruments will be keeping a close eye on atmospheric and oceanic events in the Indian and Pacific oceans. The Tropical Ocean and Global Atmosphere programme will be attempting to find the trigger for this El Nino and perhaps identify features from which another can be pre-icted, but with the enormous numbers of variables in weather and climatic forecasting that task is going to be a sticky one.

In any event, the 1982–3 El Nino was the greatest on record, so large in fact that it slowed down the rotation of the earth.

# Chance Encounters of an Earthly Kind

In the tropical rain forests of the world there is a multitude of plants and animals yet to be discovered. There may be plants valuable to medicine, animals for food and a host of creatures that may help us understand the complexities of biological communities. We are destroying that resource at an alarming rate. An area the size of Switzerland is disappearing every year.

In 'The Global 2000 Report to the President' it was estimated that a half a million to two million species worldwide are likely to become extinct by the year 2000, mostly due to habitat destruction and pollution, and that about a half to two-thirds of those are to be found in the dwindling tropical forests. The value of the genetic reservoir, says the report, is immense. Hidden in the entanglement of branches, stems and leaves are new foods, such as nuts and fruits, that could be utilised by the developing nations. There are potential medicines to be obtained from some of the plants. Wild forms of domestic species, such as strains of grasses, are important to retain, in order that disease resistance can be bred into our increasingly susceptible food plants. It's frightening to realise that four-fifths of the world's food supplies are derived from just a couple of dozen species of plants and animals.

Destruction aside, however, there are still many thousands of species, new to science, being found each year. Any excursion into a rain forest is likely to result in the discovery of several creatures as yet unidentified. There are, for example, over 275,000 known species of beetles (in fact, there are more species in the order Coleoptera than in any other order of animals) and each year several hundred new ones are added to their ranks. The chance, then, of encountering unique plants or animals in some remote part of the world, such as an unexplored rain forest, an inaccessible mountain chain, or the deep oceans, is great. Occasionally, though, such a discovery causes a considerable stir in the scientific community.

Many scientists have been ridiculed for wanting to believe in the existence of curious creatures or mythical beasts that they have heard about in legend or folklore. They have been convinced that there is an element of truth in the stories, but have been unable to substantiate their beliefs with concrete evidence. Then, quite out of the blue, a chance discovery proves that there was something in it after all, and a whole area of biological thinking must be reassessed. Often as not, the creature found is unexpected, thought to have been extinct for millions of years. It is a 'living fossil', a relic, which perhaps can be said to be out of step with evolution, but representative of life as it was millions of years ago. Such creatures are living windows on the past.

## Living fossils

Browsing through the day's catch at the Yokohama fish market, and searching for interesting specimens to sell to the world's museums, Alan Owston, an American dealer, came across an unusual type of shark. It had a long, shovel-like extension from its forehead – not as part of the upper lip like a swordfish or a sawfish – and protrusible jaws containing rows of awl-like teeth. The local fishermen, who had hauled the fish out of the Sagami-nada at the entrance of the Tokyo-Xwan, called it the goblin shark, *tenguzame*. It appears to favour deep waters, and one specimen is known only from a tooth it left embedded in a submarine telephone cable lying in 1400 metres of water in the Indian Ocean. The first specimen known to science was found in 1898. It was examined by the Japanese ichthyologist Kakichi Mitsukuri, and later by Stanford University's David Starr Jordan, an expert in Japanese fish, and given the name *Mitsukurina owstoni* in honour of its discoverers. When the scientific paper was published, however, it became clear that this was not the first time that a goblin shark had been brought to the attention of the scientific community. A fossil shark, thought to have been extinct for 100 million years, and named *Scapanorhyncus*, the shovel-snout, had already been described from fossils found in Cretaceous rock in Syria. *Mitsukurina* looked almost identical. The goblin sharks, it seems, have survived for millions of years virtually unchanged and are living proof that animals thought to have disappeared from the face of the earth may still be lurking in unexplored ecological niches unchanged for eons. And, the least-known places, safe from our prying eyes, are in the deep ocean. In 1938, the most famous of living fossils was caught in deep water off the coast of South Africa. It was the coelocanth.

The story starts at the beginning of the Devonian period, over 400 million years ago, when three distinct lines of bony fishes were evolving from the jawless, armour-plated creatures that were swimming in the sea. There were the ray-finned fishes, the Actinopterygians, that have given rise to most of the bony fishes we see today, from the herring to the marlin. The second group included the lung-fishes, the Dipnoi, that reached their peak about 350 million years ago and are represented by three 'living fossil' survivors – *Protopterus* from the African lakes, *Lepidosiren* from South America, and the very primitive *Neoceratodus* from Australia. The Crossopterygian tassel-finned fishes were the third group. They were thought to have reached their peak in the Carboniferous period, one line, the rhipsidians, having given rise to the amphibians, and another, the coelocanths, having evolved very little throughout time and possessing distinctive lobed fins and cycloid scales. The bulk of the Crossopterygian fishes died out about 60 million years ago, a few coelocanths remaining unchanged until about 20 million years ago. Then, it was thought, they too became extinct. That is, until a curious blue oily fish, about 1.5 metres long, was hauled up from about 70 metres at the mouth of the Chalumna River, near East London, in South Africa. Nothing like it had ever been seen before at East London, and so the curator of the local museum, one Miss Courtenay-Latimer, was asked to take a look at it. She was not a fish expert but, realising that it was rather unusual, brought it to the attention of Professor J. L. B. Smith of Grahamstown University, and he immediately recognised it as something special. It resembled, almost exactly, fishes that were swimming the seas from Madagascar to Greenland many millions of years ago and identified from the fossil record. It was dubbed for science *Latimeria chalumnae*, but to Smith it became known as 'Old Fourlegs'. The first specimen was caught on the 22 December 1938. The second, caught fourteen years later, almost to the day – 24 December 1952, was encountered off Anjouan, one of the Comoro Islands, in the Mozambique channel. Since then, about seventy specimens have been observed, including a living coelocanth that was filmed in shallow water and seen in the BBCtv series *Life on Earth*. Indeed, the Comoro islanders were not all that impressed with Old Fourlegs. They had been catching coelocanths for decades, one or two, on average, a year being brought up from 300 metres down. Once hooked, the fish was an infernal nuisance. It is very powerful and difficult to bring up to a small boat, such as a canoe. And, even if it reaches the surface it does not make good eating, although the rough scaly skin can be used as a kind of 'sandpaper'.

The discovery of living coelocanths showed that this particular line has changed very little for over 300 million years. Interestingly, more recent research has revealed that both the living specimens and the fossil finds contained, within the body cavity, young fish with yolk sacs, indicating that these ancient fishes were giving 'birth' to live young rather than laying eggs, a factor that might have something to do with their long-term survival.

## Megamouth

On 15 November 1976 a US Navy research ship was carrying out oceanographic work while stationary about 42 kilometres north-east of Kakuku Point, Oahu, Hawaii. To maintain their position the crew had deployed two large parachute-sea-anchors at a depth of 165 metres in waters 4600 metres deep. When the time came to move and the anchors were hauled aboard, one was curiously heavy. Trapped inside was a huge shark, 4.46 metres long and weighing 750 kilograms. Its great, blubbery lips surrounding a broad gape set on protruding jaws instantly gained it the nickname 'megamouth'. Later examination by Leighton Taylor, of the Waikiki Aquarium, Leonard Compagno, of San Francisco State University, and Paul Struhsaker, led to it being grouped, rather uneasily, with the lamnoid sharks in its own family, the Megachasmidae. It has been given the scientific name *Megachasma pelagios*, meaning large-yawning mouth of the open sea. It is thought to be a filter-feeder, and is only the third shark of this type to have been found. Morphologically and anatomically it is quite different from the basking shark and whale shark, the other filter-feeding sharks of the open ocean.

The skeleton of megamouth is composed of a soft cartilage, and the swimming muscles are thought to be sufficent for slow, steady swimming. Unlike the whale sharks and basking sharks, the largest fish in the sea, which gather food from the surface layers, the megamouth is thought to graze in the waters 150–500 metres deep. It is likely that it swims slowly through patches of *Euphausia* shrimps with jaws agape, regularly closing its mouth and contracting the pharynx to squeeze out the water and concentrate the food before swallowing it. In the stomach of the Hawaiian specimen was found a thick *Euphausia* soup.

*Euphausia* shrimps are a constituent of the zooplankton populations in the semi-dark zone, hundreds of metres below the surface. There is speculation that megamouth attracts the shrimps to its mouth with the aid of bioluminescent spots around the mouth. Silvery tissue, dotted with small circular pits, was found lining the blubbery mouth. Inside, an enormous tongue and closely packed finger-like gill-rakers were found. It may be that the tongue is used to compress the mouthful of water and food against the gill-rakers which sieve out the shrimps. The 236 tiny teeth probably help in this filtering process. In the gut was sitting a new species of tape-worm *Mixodigma leptaleum*.

On the outside of the shark was evidence of external parasites, such as the small circular bites of the voracious cookie-cutter shark. Examination of the sexual apparatus revealed megamouth to be a male. As female sharks are usually significantly bigger than males, researchers have suggested that there are even bigger megamouths swimming about down there in the deep sea.

## Monster off the Florida coast

Two young boys, crossing the beach at St Augustine, Florida in late November 1896, chanced upon the remains of a giant creature. It was partly buried in the sand. The local GP, DeWitt Webb, himself an amateur naturalist, examined the carcass, and newspaper accounts at the time describe him finding the remains of a 6-tonne octopus which measured 45 metres from the tip of one tentacle to the next when spread across the ground. This would represent the largest invertebrate to have been found anywhere in the world. Giant squid were known from the sucker marks on the sides of harpooned sperm whales and from the occasional 'kraken' washed up on beaches on both sides of the Atlantic, but this was by far the largest of them all. In fact a giant squid expert of the time, one A. E. Verrill, joined Webb in analysing tissues from the find and confirmed that it was an octopus. They submitted detailed papers on the subject but their conclusions were rejected as poppycock. It was simply a mass of blubber, they were informed, from a stranded whale. And there the matter rested until the curator of Marineland Florida, Forrest Wood, tracked down samples of the creature that had been kept in some dusty jars at the Smithsonian Institution in Washington.

Wood persuaded Joseph Gennaro of the University of Florida to analyse some of the tissues. He reported that it consisted of light and dark bands of cells similar to those seen in an octopus. In a later investigation, he sent a sample of whale tissue, recently killed squid, a piece of preserved giant squid, a chunk of ordinary octopus, and a section of the Smithsonian specimen to the University of Chicago for tissue analysis. One sample, it was reported, contained huge quantities of the supportive tissue, collagen, and this turned out to be the giant octopus sample. A very large octopus, so the explanation goes, needs some sort of support. The whale has bones and squid has elastin. A giant octopus would use collagen.

Now, the speculation is that many of these giants are likely to be found in the sea off the coast of the south-east United States, for octopuses in general lay very many eggs.

### Watch out, watch out, there's a monster about!

With two-thirds of the planet covered by sea, and most of that still to be explored, it is clear that many more surprises are still lurking in the depths. But what of the rest of the planet? Does the abominable snowman or yeti exist in the Himalayas, the Sasquatch or big-foot roam North America, and the Mono Grande climb in the Andes? Are they figments of the imagination, creatures we *want* or *need* to believe in, or are they real 'living fossils', hominid relics, survivors from the times when modern man was emerging as the naked ape?

Many giants and curious creatures have eluded the gaze of inquisitive naturalists until recent times. The Komodo dragon, for instance, was unknown to science until 1911. These enormous monitor lizards, the largest known, can grow up to 3 metres in length, the bulk of which, unlike other monitors, is in the body and not the tail. Full-grown dragons feed on wild pigs and deer, and have a particular liking for feral goats introduced to the Indonesian islands by ancient mariners. Although most food is taken as carrion, some lizards lie in wait beside goat and deer trails, seize the leg of a passing animal, throw the victim to the ground, and tear out the belly. Other cunning individuals follow a pregnant goat, grabbing the new-born kid as it drops to the ground. Since their discovery Komodo dragons have been found on several islands in the Indonesian chain, and one of their near-relatives appears to have been a giant 5-metre-long goanna which roamed the plains of Australia about 3 million years ago, long after the demise of the dinosaurs, but which itself is now extinct. Living perenty goannas at 2.5 metres from Australia, and the even longer Salvador's monitor lizard at 4 metres from New Guinea, are also recently discovered giant reptiles.

From Africa, in the early-nineteenth century, came reports of a cloven-hoofed creature that looked part zebra, part giraffe, and had horns. Sir Harry Johnson went in search of it and in 1906 gave the okapi to the world. It has a head much like a giraffe, complete with very long tongue, and its body is covered in a soft, velvety purple-black coat except for the legs and the rump, striped black and white like a zebra. This disruptive coloration is thought to give some measure of camouflage protection when fleeing from predators, such as the leopard and local pygmy tribesmen. Perhaps the most intriguing aspect of the discovery was that the okapi very closely resembled a mammal *Palaeotragus* that was thought to have been extinct 20 million years ago.

Lakes and rivers seem to be good for monsters. The Belgian naturalist Bernard Heuvelman once pointed out that, 'in the waterways of the world, anything may be possible'. St Columba stood by the side of Loch Ness in AD 565 and saw the monster, but it wasn't until the road was built just before the Second World War that the frequency of spotting increased to its present levels. Scientists equipped with underwater strobe-cameras and sonar detectors have identified Nessie-type shapes and shadows but the definitive evidence has yet to be presented. There is also 'Caddy', a sea serpent off the coast of British Columbia, 'Chessie' from Chesapeake Bay, Maryland, 'Champ' from Lake Champlain, and a host of others from lakes, bays and inlets all over the world. One suggestion is that they are not plesiosaurs, the most frequently quoted animals, but zeuglodons, primitive whale-like creatures that were thought to have been dead for 20 million years.

Could it be that large dinosaurs, other than crocodiles and birds that are thought to be the living relatives of the giant reptiles, are still to be found in places that have escaped major physical changes during the earth's history? Most of the evidence tends to be anecdotal and unconvincing, but once in a while a piece of circumstantial evidence arouses curiosities and merits investigation. Thus it was with mokele-mbembe.

## Mokele-mbembe – the search for a dinosaur

In 1776 L'Abbe Lievain Bonaventure Proyart, a Catholic missionary who worked in the Congo wrote about 'the track of an unknown animal which they did not see but which must have been monstrous: the marks of the claws were noted on the ground, and these formed a print about 90 centimetres in circumference.' The distance between prints was measured and was found to be a staggering 2.5 metres, indicating a creature the size of a small elephant, but one with gigantic claws. The locals called it mokele-mbembe.

Two hundred years later, James Powell, an authority on crocodiles, when journeying through the Gabon came across stories, told by the Fang people, about a monster known to them as n'yamala. He showed them pictures of a long-necked dinosaur which they instantly recognised as the monster for which they had a deep fear.

Mokele-mbembe and n'yamala came to the attention of University of Chicago microbiologist and tissue expert Roy Mackal, a founder member of the International Society of Cryptozoology, an organisation dedicated to seeking out bizarre and hitherto unknown animals, and a serious study to flush the monster out was embarked upon.

Mackal surveyed the literature and found that mokele-mbembe had not gone unnoticed. Trader Horn, otherwise known as Alfred Aloysius Smith, was told stories of jago-nini, the monster that lived in the swamps along the Ogooué River, in Gabon, during his excursions to Africa in the late-nineteenth century. He himself had seen frying-pan-sized, three-clawed footprints in the mud. In 1912 animal collector Carl Hagenbeck retold local stories of 'a huge monster, half elephant, half dragon' that lived 'in the depth of the great swamps', and recalled how, on the walls of several caves, he had seen drawings of the strange creature. He concluded that, 'it can only be some kind of dinosaur, seemingly akin to the brontosaurus'. He organised an expedition to search for the monster but was forced to abandon it when malaria laid the entire party low. However, the reports that impressed Mackal the most came from two German explorers.

Cameroon, prior to 1914, was a German colony, and the geographer Captain Freiherr von Stein zu Lausnitz was invited to head the Likoula-Congo Expedition of 1913 to prepare maps of this relatively unexplored region. The outbreak of war put paid to most of the work, and no report of the expedition was published. Willy Ley, a science writer, acquired what small part of the manuscript was available and translated sections that referred to a strange creature known as mokele-mbembe:

> ... at the time of our expedition a specimen was reported from the non-navigable part of the Sanga River, somewhere between the two rivers Mbaio and Pikunda; unfortunately the area could not be explored due to the brusque end of our expedition. We also heard about the alleged animal at the Ssombo River ... the animal is said to be brownish-grey with

a smooth skin, its size approximately that of an elephant . . . it has a long and very flexible neck and only one tooth, but a very long one – some say it is a horn. A few spoke of a long muscular tail like that of a crocodile. Canoes coming near it are doomed; the animal attacks vessels at once and kills the crews, but without eating the bodies . . . it lives in the caves that have been washed out by the river in the clay of its shores at sharp bends. It is said to climb the shore even at daytime in search of food; its diet is entirely vegetable. The preferred plant was shown to me. It is a kind of liana, with large white blossoms, a milky sap, and apple-like fruits. At the Ssombo River I was shown a path said to have been made by this animal in order to get at its food. The path was fresh and there were plants of the described type nearby. But since there were so many tracks of elephants, hippos, and other large mammals it was impossible to make out one particular spoor with any amount of certainty.

Von Stein's account was substantiated by that of another German explorer, Leo von Boxenberger, a retired colonial magistrate who found traces of mokele-mbembe near the mouth of the Mbam River, where it enters the Sanga in southern Cameroon during an expedition in 1938. Roy Mackal was hooked and, together with several other 'converts', undertook expeditions of his own.

He focused on an area between the Sanga and Ubangi rivers, taking account of historical reports, migrations of tribes and the encroachment of increasing river traffic. The Likouala aux Herbes River and Lake Tele, which empties into the Bai River, looked suitably remote locations, centred as they are on large patches of blank map, typical of this region. This part of the Congo consists, in fact, of vast stretches of swamplands, inhabited by mosquitoes, leeches, poisonous snakes, missionaries, and the occasional group of Binga pygmies. It is indeed, a 'lost world', virtually unexplored and unmapped, unchanged probably for the past 70 million years, and the most likely spot for a relic species to survive. Standard issue medical pack for explorers includes antidote to pygmy blow-dart poison and fourteen snake-bite sera.

Mackal went on two journeys into the Congo, each time gaining more evidence, albeit mostly circumstantial, that a strange creature lives in the region. Travel was mainly on foot or in canoes, so only small areas could be explored at a time. He carried photographs of local animals, North American ones, and a brontosaur picture to show the local people. They instantly recognised their familiar creatures, were baffled by animals like the North American bears, but picked out the brontosaur as mokele-mbembe. They said the creature frightened away hippos and 'the roar made gorillas dive for cover'.

In one story the pygmies tell of a frightening event that took place in 1959. Three of the monsters had been seen swimming in the molibos or river channels connecting Lake Tele to the Bai River. The lake is a valued fishing area where the local people catch lung-fish and perch, so a fence of wooden stakes was constructed across the four largest channels to keep the giant creatures out of the lake. One of them was reported to have charged the barrier and tried to crash through but was speared by the pygmies. They cut it into small pieces, a long job by all accounts because it was so large, and fried it up for supper. They all died.

Mackal himself found the elephant-sized, clawed footprints, together with a wide swath of bent and flattened vegetation, when he followed a track leading down to a river. He thought that the pattern could only be caused by a creature likely to be taller and larger than a crocodile. James Powell photographed a giant clawed footprint that locals said had come from the creature.

Another team of intrepid monster hunters, led by Herman Regusters, an engineer on leave from the Jet Propulsion Laboratory, and guided by a satellite receiver navigation aid, actually claim to have photographed the creature but the light was bad and as an image intensifier was unavailable the results are rather poor. They did, however, describe how the head came out of the water, travel for a quarter of a mile and dive. The animal was 'dark brownish in colour; the skin appeared to be slick and smooth; it had a long neck and a small head, which was snake-like'.

More recently, at the annual meeting of the International Society of Cryptozoology held in Paris in June 1984, Marcellin Agnagna, a zoologist assigned by the Congolese government to investigate reports of mokele-mbembe, presented details of the first well-documented sighting in Lake Tele. Agnagna believes the creature, which he watched for about twenty minutes while it lounged about just 275 metres from the lakeshore, to be one of the sauropods, a group of giant dinosaurs that were thought to have become extinct 63 million years ago and which includes the 28-metre-long *Diplodocus* and the 100-tonne, 12-metre-long

*Brachiosaurus* – two of the largest terrestrial animals ever to have lived on the planet.

The society aim to send another expedition to Lake Tele, but in the meantime Mackal and Powell have offered a $2000 reward for skeletal remains, and are convinced that there is something unknown to science living in the remote Congo. It is a mystery that still needs to be explained, for nobody has yet claimed the prize.

# Index

## Picture Credits